Acknowledgements

G000269972

I would like to thank everybody that has helped me to coll
for this book. I'd like to thank Kieran McCarthy, Sunil Sorroy, Roy Littlewood, Eric Cross, John Herdman and Jack White.

In particular, I'd like to thank Terry Sylvester, who has been a constant source of support for over three decades. Terry's knowledge of the pleasure steamer business is immense and there can be few people that possess his expertise and commitment. For almost four decades, he was the constantly enthusiastic and imaginative Commercial Director of the famous paddle steamer *Waverley*. Terry's achievements during those decades were outstanding. I'd like to thank Terry for all of the magic that he created with *Waverley* and *Balmoral* during those very special years and for always giving me huge encouragement to preserve the heritage of pleasure steamers during that time. I'd like to dedicate this book to Yvonne Gadwell, who enjoyed many happy days on *Waverley* and *Balmoral*.

It has been a pleasure and privilege to have listened to so many happy memories of the Eagle Steamer fleet over the past three decades and to be able to record these stories for posterity. It has also been gratifying to have been able to find and collect so much superb material to keep alive the memory of these special ships that were so popular in post-war years. I hope that this book is a fitting tribute to those people that enjoyed a simple and happy days aboard a Thames pleasure steamer for a carefree day at the seaside.

Introduction

If you visit the popular seaside resorts that line the long coastlines of Kent and Essex in the twenty-first century, the sight of a splendid-looking pleasure steamer arriving and disembarking hundreds of happy day trippers is a sight that few would now remember. But just half a century ago the splendid fleet of Eagle Steamers were as much a part of Margate, Southend, Clacton and Ramsgate as were the famous amusement parks such as Dreamland or the Kursaal. With such splendid names as the *Royal Sovereign, Royal Daffodil* and *Queen of the Channel,* they were as big a part of the seaside as the hugely popular shore-based attractions.

Pleasure steamer services to Kent and Essex started in the 1820s and 1830s. Many rival companies were created with the aim of dominating the Thames trade, but the mighty General Steam Navigation Company soon showed that it had the determination as well as superior paddle steamers to be number one. The early steamers were small and lacked the covered passenger accommodation that future generations would require. At the time, these services were exciting and revolutionary as steamer services cut the journey time dramatically from the old days of horse and coach travel. Railway services were developing at a similar pace, however, and so the spirit of rivalry resulted in larger and finer pleasure steamers as steam locomotives ran further into Kent and Essex. Soon, the Thames-side piers were having to be lengthened to take the larger steamers, and by the late decades of the nineteenth century the paddle steamers and seaside resorts, with their elaborate piers, had evolved to the point at which they would stay for another seventy years.

The Edwardian era witnessed a Golden Age of seaside resorts. Elaborate and exotic piers welcomed day trippers and holidaymakers to the coast after an exhilarating sea cruise. They would quickly throng the vast and similarly splendid seaside pleasure pavilions and partake of donkey rides and ice creams on the sands; the seaside resort as we know it was born. For the vast majority of people, the quickest and cheapest way to get to the seaside was aboard a pleasure steamer. This world was interrupted by the outbreak of the First World War, but by the 1920s and 1930s some of the most famous Thames paddle steamers ever built entered service when vessels such *Crested Eagle* and *Royal Eagle* took to the waters of the Thames.

By the mid-1930s, there was a move to build new tonnage that would mirror the art deco age, with streamlined shapes and the enhanced, enclosed passenger accommodation required by new generations of day trippers. The famous Denny yard of the Clyde built the first new vessel, which was regally named the *Queen of the Channel*. Soon after *Royal Sovereign* entered service and in 1939, as storm clouds formed for war, the epitome of Thames pleasure steamers entered service: the *Royal Daffodil*.

The Second World War brought with it an inevitable loss of the Thames fleet as the steamers played a major role at Dunkirk as well as acting as troop transport. With government compensation, the remaining older steamers soon had replacement vessels to run alongside the older paddle steamers. The *Royal Sovereign* and *Queen of the Channel,* along with the 1939-built *Royal Daffodil,* would dominate post-war services. Soon, demobbed servicemen joined their evacuee children for a day trip to the seaside. It seemed that the pre-eminence of seaside resorts such as Southend, Margate, Ramsgate and Clacton would last forever, but things soon started to dramatically change. After that initial buzz of rediscovering pre-war seaside delights, passengers had bigger aspirations and soon the lure of foreign holidays and the mass ownership of the motor car cast a massive and fatal blow to the famous Eagle Steamer fleet. But, those two happy decades from the end of the war until the cessation of Thames services by the General Steam Navigation Company in 1966 witnessed the heyday and golden sunset of Thames pleasure steamer services.

The *Royal Daffodil, Royal Sovereign* and *Queen of the Channel* were massive and beautifully designed ships that were perfectly suited to their happy role. Their spacious and beautifully furnished lounges provided the passenger with comfort and luxury to watch the passing coastline and shipping; no motor car could offer the same experience! Dining aboard the ships was always an adventure and a highly anticipated part of each day. Wide open decks provided passengers with ample facilities to sample the unique atmosphere of a sea cruise as the 'People's Liners' sped their way to Margate or Boulogne. But all of these attractions as well as a good number of brave initiatives by GSNC and other shipping companies could do little to halt the inevitable. By 1967, services ceased and the mighty *Royal Daffodil* was scrapped. *Royal Sovereign* and *Queen of the Channel* were also withdrawn.

The seaside resorts once visited by the Eagle Steamers soon experienced the decline that hit the steamers. Car ownership became the norm in the latter part of the twentieth century, and with the loss of many of the once glorious attractions and piers that once adorned the resorts, an integral part of the seaside had been lost forever. For many, however, the sight of a splendid pleasure steamer arriving at a seaside pier instantly reminds a generation of joyful times during those carefree post-war years aboard the pleasure steamers of the famous Eagle Steamer fleet.

THE HEYDAY OF THAMES PLEASURE STEAMERS

Andrew Gladwell

AMBERLEY

First published 2019

Amberley Publishing
The Hill, Stroud
Gloucestershire, GL5 4EP

www.amberley-books.com

Copyright © Andrew Gladwell, 2019

The right of Andrew Gladwell to be identified as the
Author of this work has been asserted in accordance
with the Copyrights, Designs and Patents Act 1988.

ISBN 978 1 4456 8069 9 (print)
ISBN 978 1 4456 8070 5 (ebook)

British Library Cataloguing in Publication Data.
A catalogue record for this book is available from
the British Library.

Typeset in 9.5pt on 11pt Celeste.
Origination by Amberley Publishing.
Printed in the UK.

An Edwardian paddle steamer alongside Margate Jetty disembarking passengers for a trip. A photo such as this gives us a real insight into what it was like on a paddle steamer in the days before the First World War. You can clearly see the purser at the gangway and the open bridge deck that was common at the time. The atmosphere wouldn't change much for another sixty years until the demise of General Steam Navigation during the mid-1960s.

The massive twin-funnelled *Royal Sovereign* at Ramsgate from an Edwardian stereoscopic slide. Ramsgate was never as popular as its neighbour Margate. It once had a railway station that ran right alongside the beach, thus providing an enticing alternative to a sometimes choppy cruise by paddle steamer.

Royal Navy warships gathered for an Edwardian Fleet Review off Margate Jetty. Such events provided an extra boost of revenue for GSNC. Paddle steamers flocked to view the warships at anchor in the Thames Estuary. Note the steps down to the tidal landing platform.

A Thames paddle steamer alongside Margate Jetty. Piers were built to facilitate the landing of paddle steamer passengers and this scene at Margate shows how busy disembarkation could be as ropes were secured and gangways moved into position. Margate had a large sign proclaiming its name. Perhaps this was a gentle reminder to those passengers that had consumed vast amounts of alcohol on the way from London!

64   MARGATE. — *View of Sands and Jetty.* — LL

Kingfisher arriving at Margate Jetty. She entered service for GSNC in 1906 and was a triple-screw steamer. Built by the Denny yard of the Clyde, she was 275 feet long. The boat deck wasn't available to passengers. With a maximum speed of 21.5 knots, she was a superb steamer for the Tilbury, Southend, Margate, Ramsgate and Deal service. She would then usually go to Boulogne or along the Kent coast to Dover.

Thames Estuary services were regularly fed by the steamers of the New Medway Steamer Packet Company. In 1924, when the company was formed, their most famous and long-lived steamer, *Medway Queen,* was built. She provided a regular link across to Southend as well as Herne Bay. The Queen Line of pleasure steamers was greatly enlivened by Captain Shippick in the 1920s. By the 1930s, it combined with the Thames-based Eagle Steamers to form the Eagle & Queen Line.

The charming little *Audrey* at Ramsgate. She was owned and operated by Captain Shippick and she became the catalyst that led to the formation of the New Medway Steam Packet Company. The well-loved Captain Tommy Aldis commanded her. Her more regular routes focussed on Southend, Herne Bay and Strood. She was very small and old-fashioned when compared to the huge motor ships that followed a decade later.

Medway Queen departing from Margate Jetty. This well-known steamer had a long career in the Thames Estuary and River Medway before being laid up in September 1963. Her career since that time has been filled with endless drama and uncertainty as she escaped the scrapyard on many occasions. Her last master was Captain Leonard Horsham.

Crested Eagle at Clacton on 12 August 1937. This photograph amply shows the wonderful foamy wake that a paddle steamer makes. Sadly for the *Crested Eagle*, her wake caused her demise as German planes were able to see it very clearly when she was bombed and sunk at Dunkirk just three years later.

1924

Special
Sunday Trips
— TO —

Southend 5/- *Return*
Giving **7** hours ashore.

Clacton - 8/-
Giving **2** hours ashore.

Children under 12 half-fare.   Under 3 no charge.

Refreshments and Afternoon Teas served on board at Popular Prices.

Leaving	Returning to Greenwich and Woolwich from	Returning to Tilbury from
GREENWICH 8 a.m.	CLACTON 3 p.m.	CLACTON 4 p.m.
WOOLWICH 8.30 „	SOUTHEND 5.15 „	SOUTHEND 6.30 „
TILBURY 9.5 „		

Passengers MUST return from Clacton by 3 o'clock Steamer, or disembark at Tilbury.

TICKETS FROM :—

THE ROYAL SOVEREIGN STEAMSHIP COMPANY'S

PIER BOOKING OFFICE.

H. Claine & Co. (London) Ltd., Printers, 88 Milton Street, London, E.C.2.

Handbill advertising special Sunday cruises from Greenwich, Woolwich and Tilbury in 1924. Sunday cruises were hugely important as most people only had Saturday afternoons off and so Sunday was often the only full day when they were able to have a cruise. Sales of liquor usually accompanied such trips, however, much to the disapproval of those that marked the Sabbath by being teetotal.

An aerial view of *Queen of Kent,* renamed in her later south coast career as the *Lorna Doone.* One of the biggest problems with the *Queen of Thanet* and *Queen of Kent* was that they didn't have large panoramic windows in the dining saloon, bars and café. This meant that passengers had a rather grim and dark dining experience, in stark contrast to all of the other pleasure steamers. The well-liked Captain Kitto was a regular master of the *Queen of Thanet.*

Handbill for cruises by the *Queen of Thanet* from Margate Jetty to view the Tongue Fort. Cruises to view the sea forts became popular from the late 1940s. Tongue Fort was positioned in the Thames Estuary in June 1942 and it was used by the Royal Navy until 1945. It soon became unstable and by the 1960s attempts were made to use it as a pirate radio station. Radio Kent was said to have started transmitting from it. *Royal Sovereign* offered similar cruises to view the forts.

Eagle and Queen Line Pleasure Steamers

P.S. "QUEEN OF THANET"

LEAVES

Margate Jetty

DAILY at 4.30 p.m.

(Fridays Excepted). Weather and other circumstances permitting.

FOR

SOUTHEND

AND

CHATHAM

FARES :

	SINGLE	SEASON RETURN
To Southend	6/-	9/-
,, Chatham	6/-	10/-

Children under 14 years half-fare

Passengers are only carried on the terms and conditions printed on the Company's Tickets.

FREE ADMISSION TO JETTY

Luggage accompanying passenger up to 100-lbs. free.

REFRESHMENTS ON BOARD   FULLY LICENSED

BOOK EARLY AT PIER HEAD

H. L. TOBY, PRINTER, MARGATE   No. 4   1947   G. V. HARTRER, Agent.

Handbill advertising trips from Margate Jetty for Southend and Chatham aboard the *Queen of Thanet*. After the Second World War the GSNC and NMSPC fleets were regarded as one body and were known as the Eagle & Queen Line.

Medway Queen, shown here on the River Medway. She provided regular cruises to Southend, Herne Bay and Clacton. She even made a charter visit to London once for preservationist Don Rose, who would later attempt to operate the *Queen of the South* on the Thames.

THE JETTY, MARGATE

Queen of Thanet and *Queen of Kent* were acquired in 1928/29 by the New Medway Steam Packet Company. They were First World War Ascot-class minesweepers and were acquired in order to expand the fleet at a time of significant growth. They were very distinctive vessels and usually provided cruises to France from Margate as well as Gravesend and Clacton. They also ventured up to Great Yarmouth, as well as to Dover.

Queen of Kent entering the harbour at Calais in the interwar years. After the end of the Second World War most of the old paddle steamers had built up a long list of necessary repairs and annual surveys, making it difficult to run them cheaply for further service. For most, the only decision was to withdraw them and lay them up or sell them in the uncertain post-war years. By 1948 and the introduction of the sleek new motor ships, the two ex-paddle minesweepers were put up for sale and were purchased by Red Funnel of Southampton for the Southampton, Isle of Wight and Bournemouth services, being renamed *Lorna Doone* and *Solent Queen*. This new career lasted only a couple of years, with both being scrapped at Dover in the winter of 1951/52.

Royal Eagle arriving at Ramsgate in the mid-1930s. She is seen here in her pale paint scheme. Note the superstructure midships as well as the steps on the sponsons that cover the paddle wheels. *Royal Eagle* had a wonderfully large sun lounge with panoramic windows that lay beneath the eagle motif on the front of the bridge.

Passengers disembarking from the *Crested Eagle* during her Thames heyday. This photograph was taken during rain and crew can be seen wearing sowesters and waterproof coats.

Crested Eagle majestically paddling along the Thames. The steamer was capable of speeds of up to 20 knots. She had horizontal venting on her paddle box, making her look a lot less attractive than other paddle steamers such as the *Golden Eagle* or *Royal Eagle*.

Crested Eagle making a confident and impressive departure from Clacton Pier on 12 August 1937. Her bridge was behind her funnel. Despite being criticised by many for her appearance, *Crested Eagle* was known for her speed and became known as the 'Greyhound of the Thames' during her career. She was built by the J. Samuel White yard at Cowes on the Isle of Wight and was perhaps the most distinctive of all the Thames paddle steamers. At 299 feet long, she was delivered ready for the 1925 season and principally operated the London to Ramsgate service. She was the first paddle steamer in the GSNC fleet to burn oil. When she was bombed at Dunkirk, the burning fuel created an inferno on the vessel.

What a sight as the *Golden Eagle* and one of the ex-First World War minesweeper paddle steamers are tied up alongside Margate Jetty in the interwar years. Margate was typical of many piers as it provided ample landing for several pleasure steamers at a time. Being mainly a destination for the steamers, it had to provide facilities that could disembark and embark many hundreds of passengers in a matter of minutes. This view shows that it was able to do its job well.

THE "CRESTED EAGLE" AND THE "ROYAL EAGLE" AT SOUTHEND PIER.

The *Crested Eagle* and *Royal Eagle* were known as the 'crack' steamers of the GSNC fleet. They looked dissimilar and provided a highly efficient and swift service from London to seaside resorts such as Southend and Margate.

"CASTING OFF."

A comic postcard produced as a souvenir and sold aboard the Eagle Steamers. Many young boys would find work on the GSNC pleasure steamers during the summer months as deckhands or in other junior roles. They would do the 101 jobs that were necessary on the steamers such as rope splicing, sweeping decks, working in the galley and of course polishing vast amounts of brass. They always wore the traditional GSNC blue seaman's jumper with 'GSNC' embroidered on the chest and wore a white flat cap. Many weren't paid for the role.

Royal Eagle at Greenwich on 18 June 1949, towards the end of her career. This view shows her tall appearance midships, where the many saloons were placed. Like most of her sisters she had a very short career of just a few years. *Royal Eagle* had a speed of around 18.5 knots, which is around 21 mph, and she could carry up to 1,987 passengers.

A paddle steamer approaches Margate Jetty with the Clifton Baths in the foreground. During the 1920s the Clifton Baths were remodelled under John Henry Iles, who also owned the Dreamland in Margate. Clifton Baths was turned into a huge and comfortable modern seaside complex with bars, cafés and restaurants on several levels and had a large open-air swimming pool reaching out into the sea. These buildings were built onto and over the remaining parts of the Clifton Baths in a neoclassical style with Mediterranean influences, laid out over a series of terraces. In 1938 the complex was renamed the Cliftonville Lido.

The bow of the *Royal Eagle* viewed from the *Crested Eagle* while alongside Southend Pier in 1938. The 1930s were important for the large paddle steamers on the Thames. Southend was always a busy place, with thousands of passengers embarking and disembarking aboard the steamers there.

Queen of Kent at Boulogne. She was a popular steamer of the Queen Line fleet. The New Medway Steam Packet Company was highly influential in the interwar years. *Queen of Kent* was a well-loved steamer at Boulogne but her career on Thames and Medway service was short.

Deckhands aboard vessels such as the *Royal Eagle* were often responsible for counting passengers on and off of each steamer at each pier. This was a very important job as vast numbers of passengers would disembark and embark upon the ships at places such as Southend. Accuracy and speed was of prime importance to ensure that passengers were transferred safely.

Royal Eagle was 1,539 tons and had a length of 292 feet. She was distinctive in that she had numerous deckhouses on the sponsons in stark contrast to steamers such as the *Crested Eagle*. She was quite small in comparison to other Thames pleasure steamers.

The *Royal Eagle* in post-war years. Many of the GSNC crew worked on the company's deep sea services during the winter months. Although busy, the summer boats were appreciated by crew as they could live closer to home. Families were often able to visit crew members on off-service days. For some crew members, they were able to go home overnight, which was very attractive to them.

Royal Eagle operated on the London Tower Pier to Southend, Margate and Ramsgate service. When the *Royal Eagle* entered service, *Crested Eagle* was put on the London Tower Pier to Southend, Clacton and Felixstowe service.

Royal Eagle alongside Southend Pier during the heyday of the Thames pleasure steamers. This view shows how important Southend Pier was to the pleasure steamers. During the 1949–50 season, 5.75 million people visited the pier. They enjoyed attractions such as the Dolphin Café, Sun Deck Theatre, Hall of Mirrors and the Solarium Café.

The first *Queen of the Channel* off London Tower Pier before the Second World War. She had been built by Denny of Dumbarton in 1935 but sadly her career was very brief as she was sunk in 1940 after being bombed.

The first and majestic *Queen of the Channel* passing the lighthouse and harbour entrance at Calais in the 1930s. The 1930s saw a significant increase in the popularity of cruises to France from the resorts of Kent and Essex.

The first *Queen of the Channel* entered service in 1935 and caused quite a stir in the Thames Estuary with her revolutionary design and immaculate looks. She was initially owned by the London & Southend Shipping Company, which was formed of the New Medway Company and Denny Brothers.

TRAVEL BY
QUEEN LINE PLEASURE STEA.

DAILY SAILINGS (Fridays Excepted)
(Weather and other circumstances permitting)

FROM LONDON TO

GRAVESEND, SOUTHEND, HERNE BAY, MARGATE BROADSTAIRS, RAMSGATE, CLACTON, WALTON FELIXSTOWE

ENJOY SUN, SEA AND FRESH AIR ALL THE WAY

From TOWER BRIDGE On and after June 8th, 1935				From GREENWICH On and after June 8th, 1935		
Destination.	MON. to THURS.	SAT.	SUN. ONLY	*Destination.*	WEEK DAYS	SUN. ONLY
TOWER PIER (Depart) a.m.	7.30	8.0	8.10	GREENWICH (Depart) a.m.	9.15	9.30
GREENWICH	8.20	8.45	8.45	N. WOOLWICH	9.45	10.0
N. WOOLWICH	8.50	9.15	9.15	GRAVESEND	10.45	11.0
GRAVESEND	9.50	10.15	10.15	SOUTHEND	11.45	12.0
SOUTHEND	11.0	11.25	11.25	HERNE BAY p.m.	1.0	1.15
CLACTON p.m.	1.0	1.25	1.25	MARGATE	2.0	2.0
WALTON	1.30	1.55	1.55	RAMSGATE (Arrive)	2.45	2.45
FELIXSTOWE (Arrive)	2.15	2.40	2.40	,, (Depart)	2.45	2.45
,, (Depart)	2.30	2.55	2.55	MARGATE	3.45	3.45
WALTON	3.15	3.40	3.40	HERNE BAY	4.45	5.0
CLACTON	4.0	4.25	4.25	SOUTHEND	6.0	6.0
SOUTHEND	6.0	6.25	6.25	GRAVESEND	7.0	7.0
GRAVESEND	7.15	7.40	7.40	N. WOOLWICH	8.0	8.0
N. WOOLWICH	8.15	8.40	8.40	GREENWICH (Arrive)	8.30	8.30
GREENWICH	8.45	9.5	9.5			
TOWER PIER (Arrive)	9.20	9.45	9.45			

Passengers for BROADSTAIRS *must* change at Margate. Thence by Granville Saloon Coach or Tram.

FARES	Day Return	Period Return	Single	Sunday	FARES	Day Return	Period Return	Single	Sunday
SOUTHEND	3/-	4/6	2/6	4/-	GRAVESEND	2/6	—	2/-	—
CLACTON	4/-	6/-	3/-		HERNE BAY	4/-	6/-	3/6	5/-
WALTON	5/-	7/-	3/6		MARGATE	4/-	6/6	3/6	5/-
FELIXSTOWE	6/-	7/6	4/-		RAMSGATE	5/-	7/6	4/6	6/-

Bank Holidays 1/- Extra. Children 6d.
No Extra Charge on Saturdays.

(Broadstairs *via* Margate 7/0 Period Return).
Children under 14 yrs. at reduced rates.

Tickets for the above Services may be purchased from the Universal Travel Bureau, 4 Charing Cross, Trafalgar Square, London, S.W.1. Phone : WHItehall 4748. Thos. Cook & Son, Ltd., Berkeley St., W.1. Phone : GROsvenor 4000. Dean & Dawson, Ltd., 7 Blandford Square, W.1. Phone : PADdington 8050.

The Continental service operated by the new luxury cross-channel liner
" Queen of the Channel," will commence on July 1st and continue throughout the season.

From Tilbury and Gravesend to OSTEND, BOULOGNE or CALAIS. Passengers from London will be conveyed to Tilbury by L.M. & S. Railway from principal stations on Fenchurch Street and St. Pancras Lines. Combined Boat and Rail Tickets now available. See separate bills for particulars, or apply to any L.M. & S. Station.

No Charge for passengers' hand luggage. Fares do not include re-admission to Piers. Parties catered for at reduced Rates. Breakfasts, Luncheons, Teas and Light Refreshments obtained on Board at Moderate charges. Dancing on Board to the latest Radio-Gram Music.

Head Office, 365/367 High Street, Rochester. Tel. Chatham 2204/5. S. J. Shippick, Managing Director.

Handbill advertising Queen Line cruises aboard the luxurious new *Queen of the Channel* from London in May 1935. Cruises operated as far as Felixstowe and Ramsgate. Just over a decade later, passengers to Margate must have been oblivious that the old timbers of Felixstowe Pier were later bought and used to repair the famous Scenic Railway at the Dreamland amusement park.

The first *Queen of the Channel*. She was hit by a bomb on 27 May 1940 and had 920 troops aboard her at the time. The bomb broke her back and the troops were taken off her by the store ship *Dorrien Rose*. She initiated a new era of pleasure steamer design on the Thames.

The first *Queen of the Channel* arriving at Margate Jetty in the late 1930s. Over 250 feet in length, she was smaller than the *Royal Eagle*. Sidney Shippick was a great innovator and relished trying new things. One change that he made was to introduce sailings on a Friday, which was normally the off-service day on the Thames.

QUEEN LINE STEAMERS
(New Medway Steam Packet Co., Ltd.)

SEASON 1936
(All sailings—Weather and other circumstances permitting)

DAILY SAILINGS
(with Exceptions as shewn)

FROM

SOUTHEND PIER

Commencing Date	Day	DESTINATION	Leaving at	Departing from
June 21st	Every Day Fridays excepted	SPECIAL TRIPS TO HERNE BAY	10.20 a.m. 3.0 p.m. *	Herne Bay 11.45 a.m. * „ 4.45 p.m. *
May 30th	Every Day	MARGATE	10.30 a.m.	Margate 4.30 p.m.
EVERY DAY, May 30th to June 20th inc.—after June 20th FRIDAYS ONLY		HERNE BAY	10.30 a.m.	Herne Bay 5.30 p.m.
		HERNE BAY Margate Ramsgate	11.10 a.m.	Ramsgate 2.40 p.m. Margate 3.40 p.m. Herne Bay 4.30 p.m.
May 30th	Every Day Fridays Excepted	CLACTON FELIXSTOWE LOWESTOFT GORLESTON YARMOUTH	11.0 a.m.	Yarmouth 9.30 a.m. Gorleston 9.50 a.m. Lowestoft 10.30 a.m. Felixstowe 2.30 p.m. Clacton 4.0 p.m.
June 21st				
May 30th	Every Day	SHEERNESS GILLINGHAM CHATHAM STROOD	11.30 a.m. 5.30 p.m. 6.30 p.m.	Strood 9.15 3.15 Chatham 9.30 3.30 Gillingham 9.45 3.45 Sheerness 10.45 4.45
May 30th	Every Day Fridays Excepted	GRAVESEND & LONDON	6.0 p.m.	Combined Boat and Rail, Period & Single Tickets issued
May 30th	Every Saturd'y & Mond'y	MARGATE & OSTEND 8 hours Ashore 2 hours Ashore	8.20 a.m.	Ostend 3.30 p.m. Margate 6.45 p.m.
May 31st	Every Sund'y & Thursd'y	MARGATE & CALAIS 7 hours Ashore 3 hours Ashore	9.50 a.m.	Calais 4.45 p.m. Margate 6.45 p.m.
June 23rd	Every Tuesday	MARGATE & BOULOGNE 8 hours Ashore 3 hours Ashore	9.0 a.m.	Boulogne 4.15 p.m. Margate 6.45 p.m.
June 24th	Every Wednesday	CLACTON & CALAIS 10 hours Ashore 3 hours Ashore	7.40 a.m.	Calais 4.15 p.m. Clacton 8.0 p.m.

* THESE SERVICES WILL **NOT** OPERATE ON **WEDNESDAYS** ON AND AFTER JULY 15th

For further information, Fares and Conditions see Overleaf.

Handbill advertising cruises from Southend Pier in 1936. By this time the Queen Line was a major player in the Thames Estuary and rivalled GSNC through its rapid and impressive interwar period expansion. Boulogne and Calais offered more exotic destinations than Margate and Clacton, but at three times the fare this wasn't an option for everyone.

The first *Royal Sovereign* was built for the New Medway Steam Packet Company by Denny of Dumbarton and was launched on 28 May 1937. By the time of her delivery, the New Medway Steam Packet Company had been acquired by the General Steam Navigation Company. The name *Royal Sovereign* was chosen to coincide with the accession and coronation of George VI. At the outbreak of the Second World War, the *Royal Sovereign* was initially used for the evacuation of women and children from riverside towns in Essex and Kent to the safer area of East Anglia. She later saw service as a troop carrier between Southampton and Cherbourg before being lost.

The pre-war *Queen of the Channel* departing from Margate around 1938. The Thames motor ships of the 1930s and 1940s flared out in the middle to mimic the wide sponson area that paddle steamers had. This extra width enabled the ships to have larger and more comfortable passenger accommodation.

The first *Queen of the Channel* at Le Courgain maritime at Calais in the interwar years. This maritime area was heavily rebuilt after the war. Fish was sold from named booths on the quayside from boats bearing the same name. Behind is a lighthouse, which was built in 1848 to replace a lantern in the lookout tower.

The first *Queen of the Channel.* Her career was very short but during those few years she was an example of what the future held on the Thames. When the liner *Queen Mary* had its maiden voyage from Southampton in May 1936, the *Queen of the Channel* provided a celebratory excursion from the River Medway to Southampton to mark the inaugural sailing.

The stern of the *Royal Sovereign* showing the side 'blisters' that enabled the vessel to have excellent and commodious passenger accommodation. What a glorious sight *Royal Sovereign* made when she departed from a pier for a delightful day of cruising!

Royal Daffodil's inaugural season was intended to offer trips to the Continent from London Tower Pier. She was quickly requisitioned for war service and spent the initial days and weeks evacuating children from Kent, London and Essex to East Anglia. When the *Royal Daffodil* transported evacuees to the safety of the east coast, there was great excitement during the cruise as word spread that an enemy submarine had been spotted. Hundreds of children crowded the rails on one side of the steamer looking to the water to see it, but the rumours were untrue.

Royal Daffodil was built by the famous Denny yard at Dumbarton and had diesel engines. She was launched on 24 January 1939 and entered service in May 1939. Inevitably after such a busy war, the *Royal Daffodil* needed a total refit at the cessation of hostilities. Her most familiar post-war cruises were from Gravesend or Tilbury to view the French coastline, as well as sometimes calling at Southend and Margate.

Royal Eagle on her first trip of the season, arriving at Southend Pier on 1 July 1950. At the end of the war many paddle steamers were laid up and later scrapped. Just six ships were available for further service against thirteen that had been available at the outbreak of the war. It was felt that there was a need for a large fleet again as Eagle & Queen Line were supremely optimistic that the pre-war queues would return, especially with the large number of demobbed soldiers and their families wanting a day at the seaside again.

For many Londoners a trip aboard an Eagle Steamer pleasure steamer such as the *Royal Eagle* was a rare opportunity for a day out. It was often said that market porters from Smithfield and Billingsgate went down into the bar as soon as they boarded at London Tower Pier, eventually emerging as they arrived back at the pier some twelve hours later. They would universally say how much they enjoyed the sea and Margate, having been below decks for the entirety of the cruise!

Dining aboard the Eagle Steamer fleet was managed with military precision. Diners were able to book their meal slot and had to arrive in the dining saloon at precisely the right time. After consuming favourites such as fish and chips or steak pie, they were quickly hurried out so that the next diners could be seated and processed. Most passengers were unaware of how much work was involved in getting stores aboard the ship each day.

Royal Eagle must be regarded as something of a transition vessel; she bridged the gap between the older paddle steamers such as the *Golden Eagle* and the new motor ships such as the *Queen of the Channel*. Fried fish was a great favourite among diners, but they could also have dishes such as lobster or cold meat salads. Dining was usually according to class and the more discerning diners were offered more elaborate dishes.

A view of *Royal Eagle* in her heyday. Capable of carrying up to 1,966 passengers, she was present at Dunkirk and was later employed as a 'flak' ship in the Thames Estuary. *Golden Eagle* was sold to T. W. Gray to be broken up in 1951, while her younger sister *Royal Eagle* was sent for scrapping in November 1953. She had been laid up since 1950 in Whitewall Creek on the River Medway. It was a sad end for two glorious Thames paddle steamers.

Royal Daffodil at Boulogne. *Royal Daffodil* undertook a number of school trips from Calais to London with French schoolchildren before the start of the main 1966 season. *Royal Daffodil* was perfectly suited to the cross-Channel cruises to France from London and arriving back at Tilbury.

Queen of Kent (front) and *Queen of Thanet* (rear) moored at Calais in the interwar years. After these two old vintage paddle steamers had been disposed of, P. & A. Campbell were in conversation with Eagle & Queen Line in 1951 to place either the *Royal Eagle* or *Golden Eagle* for south coast cruising out of Brighton. This sadly came to nothing as the operating costs were deemed to be too high to make the service economic.

Royal Sovereign at London Tower Bridge. *Royal Sovereign* was the last of the Thames pleasure steamers to survive. After being withdrawn from service she became a ferry and survived for several more decades, albeit vastly transformed.

Queen of the Channel at Boulogne. For many years the master of the *Queen of the Channel* was Captain Peter Stoddard; the Bosun was Mr Jenkins and the First Officer was Mr Mann. Apart from her connection with France, *Queen of the Channel* had the honour of being the first pleasure steamer to call at the new Deal Pier.

Queen of the Channel at Calais. These cruises ran on most days of the week from Margate, Ramsgate and Deal for 37s 6d return. The New Medway Steam Packet Company merged with the General Steam Navigation Company in the late 1930s, and after the former Mersey ferry *Royal Daffodil* was withdrawn, the new 1939 motor ship took her name.

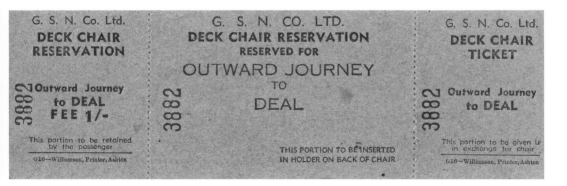

Deckchair reservation ticket issued by GSNC for a cruise to Deal. Passengers could reserve a deckchair for a fee of a shilling. Passengers had to place the central portion at the back of the deckchair to show that they'd paid the fee. Eagle Steamers were very good at getting every last penny from passengers on a day trip. Deckhands would also strategically place an upturned cap alongside the deckchairs to collect lucrative tips.

Queen of the Channel at Boulogne. The Basilica of Notre Dame was a prominent landmark at Boulogne. Many trippers would enjoy a browse along the Rue de Lille while on a day trip or visit the famous Belfry or Boulogne Castle. The town offered plenty to do during the few hours ashore.

Royal Daffodil arriving at Boulogne on 27 July 1958. It was common for passengers to sing in unison as they approached a pier, and on the *Royal Daffodil* they often sang 'Now is the Hour'. Frank Cawthron was Chief Steward aboard the *Royal Daffodil* for many years.

Queen of the Channel sweeping majestically into Boulogne with a full load of passengers during her last few years of Thames service. GSNC were fully confident that France was their best option for high revenue in those final years and no evidence exists to show that they looked closer to home to exploit new patterns of operation.

S   353

THE GENERAL STEAM NAVIGATION COMPANY, Ltd.

AVAILABLE DAY OF ISSUE ONLY.

TOWER PIER to CLACTON (VICE-VERSA)

Eagle Steamers usually issued small card tickets with various colour combinations, but this one is a thin paper one, so it may have been for a special charter to Clacton from London.

SINGLE.

Does not admit to Sun Deck Enclosure.

THIS TICKET TO BE GIVEN UP ON LANDING.

THIS TICKET IS ISSUED SUBJECT TO THE COMPANY'S CONDITIONS PRINTED ON THEIR SAILING BILLS, LEAFLETS AND NOTICES.

35

Royal Daffodil leaving France for home in the late 1950s. In the early 1960s, Jerry Lee Lewis entertained passengers aboard the *Royal Daffodil*. On one memorable cruise over 800 rockers, twisters and jivers paid £5 7s 6d for the music-packed cruise from Southend to Boulogne where the mayor greeted them. At Boulogne there was a shore-based Teen-Beat Show at the Casino with French, English and American stars ready to perform. The Outlaws performed along with Jerry Lee. Unfortunately, many English teenagers consumed vast amounts of alcohol on the way to France and were hell-bent on re-enacting the Battle of Agincourt on the beach. People were chased back to the *Royal Daffodil* and Jerry Lee Lewis, as well as 'Nero and the Gladiators', had great trouble getting back to the ship in the time. Things were made worse as the master of the *Royal Daffodil* wanted to flee. When the *Royal Daffodil* left the port, English teenagers threw glass bottles at the French youths on the quayside. The following day the *News of the World* had the headline 'Jazz Boat Kids Riot'. On the way home Jerry Lee Lewis performed for well over an hour and gave what was said to be one of his finest performances ever.

The bow of the *Medway Queen* during her preservation era. She has now spent more of her career in preservation than in service. *Medway Queen's* final trip was on 8 September 1963 when she made emotional civic farewells at her old calling points of Herne Bay and Southend. It was said at her withdrawal that over £4,000 would be required to carry out the necessary maintenance work to prolong her service; that simply wasn't an option. Her withdrawal caused a huge public outcry in the press and a series of articles were run in the London evening newspapers. These articles emphasised her noble exploits at Dunkirk but it was simply too late to do anything. The *Evening News* articles had some effect, however, as her owners decided to save her rather than to send her for scrap. She was sold to the Forte hospitality empire for static use. Her life after 1963 has been more eventful (and longer) than her Thames and Medway career.

Royal Daffodil at Southend Pier. Her name was perhaps a little odd in that it didn't fit in with the names of her two sister motor ships, who she joined in 1939. Her name was more suited to the River Mersey and Liverpool, where her predecessor had originated from.

The impressive passenger accommodation aboard the *Royal Daffodil*. She could accommodate up to 2,073 passengers. It became clear just a few years after the end of the war that the initial optimism was an illusion and that Thames pleasure steamer services were going to be hugely affected by changes in taste as for the first time people realised that they had new options. It was difficult for Eagle & Queen Line to react to the situation as it was clear that they were entering into the unknown; their 130 years of experience in the business couldn't give them a clear view of the future.

The cocktail bar aboard the *Royal Sovereign*. Many of the crew employed by Eagle Steamers worked in the bars and restaurants of top London hotels during the winter months. Work on the pleasure steamers was purely a summer job. The usual off-service day was on Friday, and Saturday was of course the busiest day of the week.

Royal Sovereign moored adjacent to the Traitor's Gate at the Tower of London. The famous landmark and nearby Tower Bridge provided the most amazing and exciting sight for steamer passengers at the start or end of each cruise. However rough the day at sea may have been, the sight of Tower Bridge floodlit at night provided the most majestic end to each day.

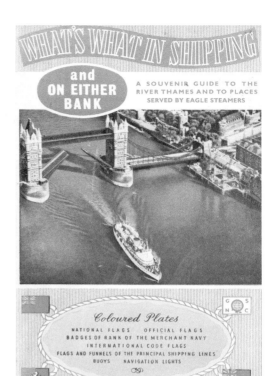

The cover of the small booklet named 'What's What in Shipping', which was sold around the decks of the GSNC motor ships during the post-war years. These little guides proved to be very popular with passengers as they explained many of the features and ships during the journey to the seaside resorts.

Royal Daffodil at London. Music cruises were an initiative to increase business for Eagle Steamers as well as to appeal to a new and emerging market – the teenagers. Many of the musicians were managed by Don Arden, who was the father of TV celebrity Sharon Osbourne. Live entertainment was offered by the top stars of the day. Jerry Lee Lewis performed onboard in 1963 while Gene Vincent was another artiste in 1962. Although these initiatives were an excellent idea, they proved unprofitable. Many of the artists have since remarked how memorable the cruises were because of stormy seas; seasickness often gave them negative memories of the *Royal Daffodil*!

Queen of the Channel's sailings in May 1949 included cruises from Ramsgate to France or along the Kent coast to Dover with an onward cruise towards Dungeness. She later took on the London Tower Pier to Clacton service, calling at Southend.

A view of *Royal Daffodil*'s bridge on 19 August 1952. *Royal Eagle* was the first Thames pleasure steamer to re-enter service in 1946 on her well-loved and popular London Tower Pier to Southend and Margate run.

Royal Daffodil approaching Margate Jetty. Margate and Cliftonville were lucky in that the pleasure steamers could be viewed from the shore. The excitement of the whistles and hundreds of happy holidaymakers arriving at Margate provided a perfect advertisement for a sea cruise.

The first issue of *Seacruse* magazine sold aboard Eagle & Queen Line pleasure steamers in August 1948. The company was excellent in promoting their steamers. By publishing a guide like this, they were able to provide a huge amount of information to entice passengers on future cruises in the days before smartphones. Each guide included information about each steamer as well as places that could be visited.

THE MEN WHO GET YOU THERE—

★

Drawings by **MICKEY DURLING**, Southend Pier Sketch Artist.

6

Masters of the Eagle Steamers fleet from the 1948 magazine. Captain Paterson was in command of the *Royal Daffodil*. He was with the *Royal Daffodil* during the Second World War and was awarded the Distinguished Service Cross for services at Dunkirk. During the conflict, the vessel steamed around 170,000 miles and carried 2,443,979 service and civilian passengers. Captain Kitto commanded the *Golden Eagle*. In 1939 he evacuated children from London to the east coast aboard the *Queen of the Channel*. After a busy war he was awarded the Distinguished Service Cross and was mentioned in despatches four times. Captain Traynier commanded the *Royal Eagle*. In 1939 he evacuated 3,000 children and their mothers from Dagenham and Tilbury to Great Yarmouth aboard the *Golden Eagle*. He ended the war on *Golden Eagle* on the River Sheldt and at Antwerp, maintaining balloon barrage. Captain Kelly was master of the *Queen of Thanet*. He spent the war on the east coast. Captain Leonard Horsham was master of the *Medway Queen*. He spent some of the war on minesweeping duties along the east coast. Captain Aldis was master of the *Queen of Kent*. In 1939, he commanded the *Royal Sovereign* when she evacuated children from London to the east coast. He was aboard the *Royal Sovereign* when she sunk during the conflict and he was badly injured. He was awarded the Lloyd's Medal and was mentioned in despatches. In 1941 he joined the *City of Rochester* when she was blown up by a mine in the Medway.

Royal Daffodil was used to carry troops of the British Expeditionary Force to France from mid-September to October 1939. Being so large in size and new, she was particularly attractive to the Royal Navy. She took part in the Dunkirk evacuation in 1940. Many of her post-war passengers must have remembered those challenging days.

WHERE THE STEAMERS GO, & WHEN.

From **LONDON** [TOWER PIER & GREENWICH] **DAILY** [FRIDAYS EXCEPTED] to
SOUTHEND, MARGATE, RAMSGATE, CLACTON

			" Golden Eagle "	" Royal Eagle "
TOWER PIER	dep. a.m.		8.15	9.00
GREENWICH	,, ,,		8.45	9.30
SOUTHEND	arr. ,,		11.15	Noon
MARGATE	,, p.m.			2.00
RAMSGATE	,, ,,			* 2.40
CLACTON	,, ,,		2.00—3.00	
,,	dep. ,,		3.00—4.00	
RAMSGATE	,, ,,			* 2.45
MARGATE	,, ,,			3.30
SOUTHEND	,, ,,		6.00	5.30
GREENWICH	arr ,,		8.30	8.00
TOWER PIER	,, ,,		9.00	8.30

On Saturdays and Sundays only.   (Times of return will be advanced early in September.)

FARES from LONDON

	Single		Day Return Mon. Tue. Sat./Sun. Wed. Thur B.Hol.		Period Return	
To	G/E	R/E	G/E	R/E	G/E	R/E
SOUTHEND	6/-	6/-	7/6	9/-	7/6	9/-
MARGATE	12/-	15/-	18/-			18/-
RAMSGATE	13/-	16/-	20/-			20/-
CLACTON	11/-		*14/-	16/-	16/-	

* Also Saturdays.

On **Saturdays, Wednesdays and Thursdays**—M.V " CRESTED
   EAGLE "—PORT OF LONDON RIVER AND DOCK CRUISES.
   From Tower Pier at 2.30 p.m.——**Advance Bookings Only.**
On **Sundays, Mondays and Tuesdays**—M.V " CRESTED EAGLE."
   From Tower Pier at 2.30 p.m., Greenwich at 3.00 p.m.
   For a Cruise down the Thames towards Gravesend.   Arr back
   Greenwich about 6.00 p.m., Tower, 6.30 p.m.   Fare—**7/6**
From **GRAVESEND** (West St.) **PIER**—M.V " ROYAL DAFFODIL,"
at 9.00 a.m.——SOUTHEND, 10.00 a.m.——MARGATE, 12.15 p.m.
For a Channel Cruise along the French Coast :

FARES

from **GRAVESEND, 20/-** ,   **SOUTHEND, 16/-** ,   **MARGATE, 12/6**

★

Children—from **3 to 14 years, Half Fare ;** under **3 years, Free.**
**ALL SAILINGS SUBJECT TO WEATHER AND OTHER
CIRCUMSTANCES PERMITTING**
Passengers are carried only upon the Terms and Conditions printed on the
G.S.N. and N.M.S.P Companies' Tickets.
FOR FURTHER DETAILS SEE BILLS ON PIERS
40

From SOUTHEND-ON-SEA PIER

Dep. at	To	Hours Ashore	Day Return Mon./Thurs.	Sat./Sun. & B.Hol.	Period Return
	" Royal Daffodil "				
10.00	MARGATE	5½	9/-	11/-	11/-
	FRENCH COAST	—	16/-	16/-	—
	" Queen of Kent "				
10.15	MARGATE	3½	7/6	9/-	9/-
	" Rochester Queen "				
10.30	HERNE BAY	5	6/-	6/-	9/-
	" Golden Eagle "				
11.15	CLACTON	2¾	7/6	10/-	10/-
	" Medway Queen "				
11.20	SHEERNESS	4	5/-	5/-	6/-
	CHATHAM	2	6/6	6/6	9/-
	ROCHESTER	1½	6/6	6/6	9/-
	" Royal Eagle "				
12.00	MARGATE	1½	9/-	11/-	11/-
	RAMSGATE	—	—	12/-	12/-
	" Queen of Thanet "—Mondays and Wednesdays.				
3.00	CRUISE TO NORE FORTS	4/-			
4.15	MARGATE				9/-
	RAMSGATE				10/-
	" Royal Eagle "				
5.30	LONDON		Single, 6/-		
	" Royal Daffodil "				
7.30	GRAVESEND		,, 3/6		

From MARGATE PIER

On Mondays and Wednesdays.
" Queen of Thanet "

11.15	SOUTHEND	3	7/6		9/-
	Daily (Fridays excepted) " Royal Daffodil "				
12.15	CHANNEL CRUISE		12/6	12/6	
	" Queen of Kent "				
2.30	TONGUE FORTS	Fare, 4/-			
	" Royal Eagle "				
3.30	SOUTHEND		Single, 7/-		11/-
	LONDON		,, 12/-		18/-

From RAMSGATE HARBOUR

" Queen of Thanet "
On Sundays, Tuesdays and Thursdays

10.20	DOVER		6/6		

From CLACTON PIER

" Golden Eagle "

3.00-4.00	SOUTHEND		Single ·7/-		10/-
	LONDON		,, 11/-		16/-

FOR FURTHER DETAILS SEE BILLS ON PIERS.
41

List of departures along with fares for the 1948 season. Within a few years, old-timers *Golden Eagle* and *Royal Eagle* were withdrawn from service. In 1948, people were optimistic about the future of Thames pleasure steamers, but very soon reality overtook initial heavy passenger use as people fell in love with the motor car, which gave them independence.

"Will you ask the Manager on the Verandah if he thinks I'll be Sea-Sick."

A cartoon from the 1948 *Eagle Steamer* magazine, concerning seasickness. Rough seas often ensured that passengers regretted their trip to France. *Royal Sovereign* later gained a horrendous reputation when she operated cross-Channel ferry services as *Autocarrier*.

Royal Eagle at Southend Pier. *Royal Eagle* was built at Birkenhead and was one of the most distinct paddle steamers of the Thames fleet. She was commanded by Captain Bill Branthwaite, who was larger than life, making him a familiar and well-loved character for passengers. Many often returned year after year to their favourite ship to see familiar crew and officers who were regarded as friends.

The wonderful 1951 'Festival of Britain' provided a fair bit of extra business for the almost-new fleet of GSNC pleasure steamers. The festival was located on the South Bank and provided a glimpse of the exciting and colourful world that lay ahead for those that had recently been through the Second World War. A day at Margate or Southend must have been a wonderful treat to coincide with a visit to the festival.

MARGATE PIER

The three post-war motor ships were very popular with group bookings. Most large companies at the time would arrange an outing for their staff once a year and the seaside resorts of Margate and Southend were natural magnets for the group trade. Obviously, such cruises were often lively affairs. Once they arrived at the resorts, popular attractions such as Dreamland at Margate offered great potential for mass catering, where up to 3,000 people could be catered for at one sitting in the Garden Café and Sunshine Café.

SCENIC VIEW
Cocktail
COASTER

CUT ON DOTTED LINE

A postcard that could also be used as a stylish cocktail coaster showing the *Royal Sovereign* in the early 1960s. On Saturdays, Sundays, Tuesdays and Wednesdays from 1949 to 1954, *Royal Daffodil* ran the Gravesend to Southend and Margate cruise and then on to view the French coastline. On Thursdays and Mondays, she cruised to Dover or Folkestone.

45

Royal Sovereign approaching Southend Pier on 8 September 1963. Look at the large number of passengers on deck watching the excitement of the approach to the famous pier. Most would be getting off to sample the delights of the famous Kursaal and Peter Pan's Playground.

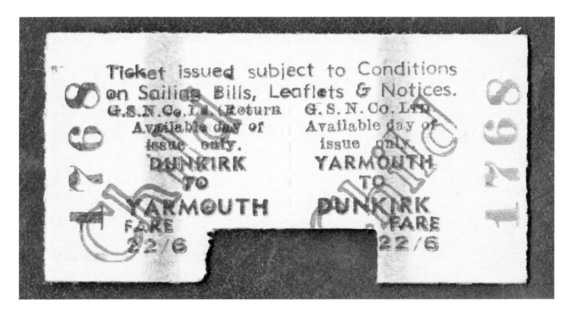

Great Yarmouth was used in 1966 as an embarkation point for the *Royal Sovereign* for cross-Channel trips to Calais as well as for local trips. At the end of that year on 20 December 1966, GSNC made the monumental announcement that their Thames excursion services were ceasing.

The purser aboard the GSNC motor ships always had a huge number of card tickets in a rack. They were brightly coloured and usually had bold coloured stripes on them to show a different design for each cruise, destination, passenger or journey types. This ticket was for a child return from Deal to Boulogne.

The *Queen of the Channel* making an impressive arrival at Boulogne during the 1960s.

Royal Daffodil at Margate. *Royal Daffodil* was 299 feet 7 inches long and was 50 feet wide. She had a gross tonnage of 2,060. Chas Hodges of the Cockney singing duo Chas & Dave often performed on the *Royal Daffodil* during the early 1960s.

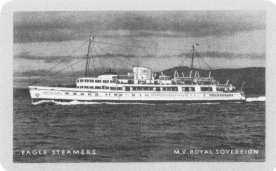

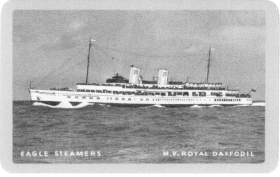

Souvenir playing cards sold featuring the motor ships. The three GSNC motor ships were similar to countless other paddle and pleasure steamers built around the UK at the end of the war to replace wartime losses. All were almost new when they were scrapped or withdrawn from service and could have had long operational careers. Their owners presumed that the pre-war boom would continue after the war, but the onward march of the motor car and television had such a profound effect on British life that these steamers were unfit for the new age.

Rochester Queen was a versatile little vessel. A regular run was to Herne Bay from Southend, where passengers could catch an East Kent bus to nearby Canterbury. The journey by car or train would have been considerable, but it was just one hour and forty minutes away by ship.

STEAMERS AT THE PIER HEAD, SOUTHEND-ON-SEA.

The well-loved *Royal Sovereign* viewed from an approaching pleasure steamer in the early post-war years. The arrival or departure at Southend encapsulates the excitement and anticipation of a pleasure steamer cruise. It was always a hive of activity and provided more than ample excitement for people soaking up the sun along the long sun decks. Southend's landing facilities have many levels to cater for the large tidal range of the Thames.

Towards the end of her career in 1966, *Royal Sovereign* was based at Great Yarmouth and undertook English Channel cruises to Calais. This wasn't a great success, perhaps due to the superior accommodation of the car-carrying vehicle ferries that were emerging at the time.

Royal Sovereign moored in front of the Tower of London during the 1950s. This aerial image shows the City of London in the days before the skyscrapers that we know today. Instead, St Paul's Cathedral dominates the London skyline. Note the numerous Thame-side wharves opposite the *Royal Sovereign* and the wartime bomb damage around St Paul's. The city skyline changed dramatically from the 1960s onwards and passengers from the time of this photo would find it hard to recognise the skyline today.

A busy start of the day in London as the *Royal Sovereign* is seen passing under Tower Bridge. The *Royal Eagle* lies alongside Tower Pier, waiting to embark more passengers. The start and end of each day required huge effort as thousands of passengers and many tons of stores such as beer, meat and vegetables had to be loaded quickly.

Royal Sovereign had a wonderful covered observation lounge on her sun deck and a very spacious and luxurious lounge on her promenade deck. She was launched on 7 May 1948 and completed her maiden cruise on 24 July, sailing from London Tower Pier to Ramsgate.

Above left: Southend Pier was always a natural magnet for ship lovers who loved to watch the arrival and departure of vessels such as the *Royal Sovereign*. She offered a very popular cruise to Margate, which was a long journey by car or train. The two hours ashore enabled passengers to enjoy Dreamland or the Lido.

Above right: Wednesdays were often popular days aboard the Eagle Steamers as in the 1950s and 1960s a great many shops closed for half-day trading. It was a time when most shopworkers still had to work on Saturdays, so time off was limited. Three butchers from Gravesend – one of whom was Bill Russell – were often seen leaning against the handrails on their weekly cruise, discussing the cruise and butcher business.

Published by

THE GENERAL STEAM NAVIGATION CO. LTD.

(EAGLE STEAMERS)

THREE QUAYS, TOWER HILL, LONDON, E.C.3.

Mincing Lane 3000

Price Two Shillings

The three GSNC motor ships at Southend from the *Eagle Steamers* guide. When the sparkly new post-war *Royal Sovereign* and *Queen of the Channel* entered service, it was inevitable that older paddle steamers would depart swiftly for the breakers' yard or service elsewhere. *Queen of Kent* and *Queen of Thanet* quickly left the Thames fleet due to their age and condition. They had been regarded as being uneconomic before the start of the war, so it was inevitable that they would be first to go. Both of these ex-Admiralty vessels saw further service for Red Funnel at Southampton.

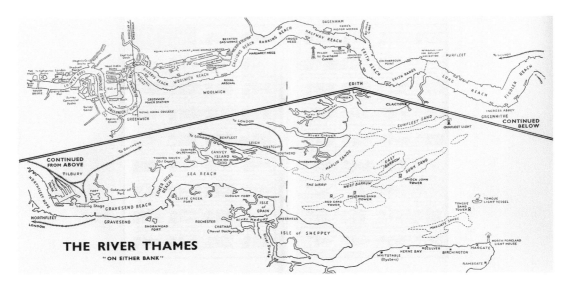

The routes operated by Eagle Steamers during the 1950s. From 1957 until the early 1960s there were few changes in the pattern of Thames sailings by the company.

Disembarkation of passengers from the *Queen of the Channel* at Boulogne. What a relaxed scene with little security and the GSNC tent in evidence as passengers spend a few hours ashore to enjoy France. Note the open sun lounge beneath the bridge with its many deckchairs and the wonderfully designed covered and open decks around the central enclosed accommodation.

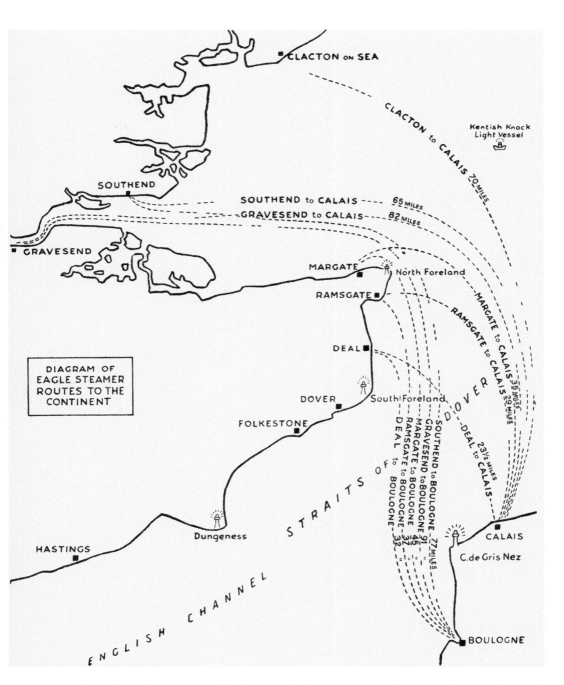

A map from the *Eagle Steamer* guide showing the distance in miles between the UK and French destinations. The landing and non-landing trips were obviously greatly affected by the rise in popularity of the cross-Channel ferries during the late 1950s and early 1960s. The vast array of services, eateries and shops aboard the ferries were in stark contrast to the GSNC motor ships. People's requirements were also changing, and with increased consumerism it was now important for people to do more than sit in a deckchair. The ability to take their car on a trip was another obvious attraction.

Royal Daffodil in her heyday. *Royal Daffodil's* final Thames season was in 1966. Soon after the announcement by GSNC that Thames services would cease she was towed away to Gwent by tug along the Terneuzen Canal. Her final sad voyage was filmed by the BBC. Although missed by a legion of fans, people felt that the other two vessels would carry on in some form.

Royal Daffodil's initial post-war service was from Gravesend to the French coast, with stops at the lucrative piers of Southend and Margate. This ticket, which was used by a member of a school outing, dates from the late 1950s, when she was able to land passengers at Calais again.

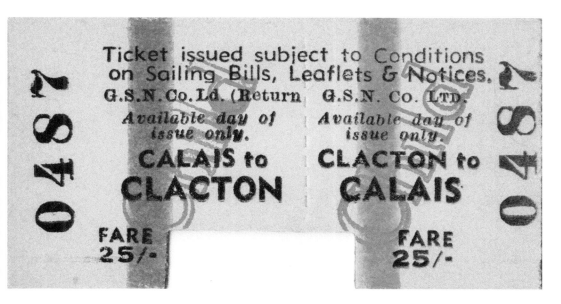

A return ticket for a cruise between Clacton and Calais. The Essex resort was never as popular as Southend and Margate due to its size and location. It was used in the latter years of the pleasure steamers to try and garner some extra income as services elsewhere contracted.

Queen of the Channel at Boulogne. After the Second World War it took around ten years before the pleasure steamers could call again at Boulogne and Calais as wartime mines had to be cleared. Cruises along the coastline of France were often provided.

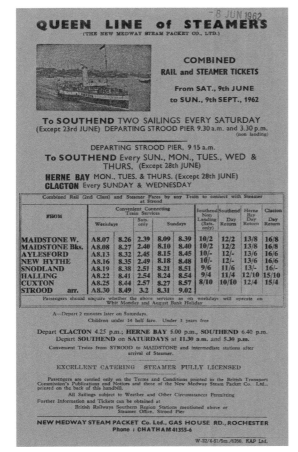

Above: Ramsgate was an attractive calling point for steamers such as the *Queen of the Channel*, seen here at Boulogne. It was said that many galley boys discarded GSNC plates and crockery out of galley portholes at Ramsgate when they got tired of their role!

Left: The *Medway Queen* was thirty-eight years old in 1962 and carried passengers from the Medway towns to Southend, Herne Bay and Clacton. She was significantly different to the three GSNC motor ships. Finding passengers from Medway was often problematic. Connecting train and bus services from places such as Maidstone and Aylesford to Strood provided excellent links to the nearby Strood Pier and combined train and steamer tickets were attractive to passengers.

Herne Bay Pier suffered damage during the 1953 floods and by the 1960s the pier was suffering from structural defects and ceased taking pleasure steamer passengers. On 11 January 1978 winter storms damaged the main pier structure, leaving only the landing stage and pier head standing isolated out at sea, as shown in this image.

The Queen of the Channel alongside the massive Prince George Extension at Southend Pier. This view shows the massive length of the pier as well as showing how superb the berthing facilities were as two huge pleasure steamers could be berthed along the front face at the same time.

Queen of the Channel moored off Tower Pier on 23 July 1954. *Queen of the Channel* was once looked at as a second vessel to support the *Waverley* but wasn't right for the role. *Balmoral* was ultimately purchased to become *Waverley's* consort.

The late 1950s and early 1960s saw the *Royal Sovereign* run the London Tower Pier to Southend and Margate service. Passengers were also able to embark at Margate for shorter coastal cruises. At the same time, *Royal Daffodil* was operating the no-passport trips from Gravesend and Southend onward to Boulogne and Calais. Various short coastal cruises were also offered by the steamer. At the same time, *Queen of the Channel* embarked passengers at Clacton or Margate, Ramsgate and Deal for cruises to France.

Queen of the Channel moored at London. Gravesend was one of the first calling points. The well-known Aubrey Loft was the agent for the Eagle Steamers in Gravesend and sold vast numbers of tickets for the steamers right up to the end of Thames services in the 1960s from his shops in New Road and Windmill Street. Handbills were placed outside of his shops. The importance of such agents was crucial to the success of pleasure steamer services as they had immense knowledge of local trade.

The second *Royal Sovereign* was quite similar to her predecessor. Improvements included a covered observation lounge on the sun deck and a spacious lounge on the promenade deck. At either end of the main deck were two dining rooms, seating ninety-six and 140 persons respectively.

Royal Daffodil departing from Southend Pier. The pier is the longest pleasure pier in the world. This was due to the fact that Southend has a muddy shallow foreshore and it was necessary to build a pier more than a mile from the shore.

Margate Jetty as it was known to countless millions of pleasure steamer passengers during the Thames heyday. The jetty was designed by the most famous of all pier designers, Eugenius Birch. At the pier head there were cafés, shops and waiting rooms to cater for passengers. Birch came from London and designed fourteen seaside piers between 1853 and his death in 1884. The cast-iron posts of his piers were revolutionary in design as they were screwed rather than being hammered into the seabed. This gave greater strength and a long life.

Above: *Royal Sovereign* departing from Margate Jetty during the 1960s. The foreground shows the future in the shape of the motor car, which would soon dominate life and the seaside. Within little more than a decade after this photograph was taken, both the *Royal Sovereign* and the jetty had gone from Margate.

Right: Monday was known as 'Eagle Steamers Night' at Dreamland. It was held in the Dreamland Ballroom between 7.45 and 11.00 p.m. Dancers could win tickets for Channel cruises from the resort. Dancing cost 3s 6d and they danced to Ray Gordon and his Dreamland Orchestra.

ENTERTAINMENTS, CINEMAS, ETC.

DREAMLAND
WELCOMES YOU
Tel. THANET 21212

AMUSEMENT PARK
Open all day and every day ● 20 acres of thrilling fun !

THURSDAY, 25 JULY - (On FRIDAY if rain prevents Display)
HUGE DISPLAY OF
BROCK'S FAMOUS FIREWORKS
Admission to Park after 6 p.m.   Adults 1/   Children 6d.
Grandstand (6,000 Seats) 6d. extra.

Nightly at Dusk   A Brilliant Holiday Spectacle
THE FIVE-ACRE **ILLUMINATED MAGIC GARDEN**
FULLY LICENSED SWISS BEER GARDEN
Adults 1/-   -   Children 6d.

CONT DAILY from 2. p.m.   **THE CINEMA**   SUNDAY CONT from 3 p.m.
CHILDREN'S MATINEE EVERY SATURDAY at 10 a.m.
Fri. & Sat. 19 & 20 July **BOY ON A DOLPHIN** ⓊCinemascope Eastman Colour
SUNDAY, 21 July   Cont. from 3 p.m.   L.C.P. 7.5 p.m.
Rock HUDSON, Yvonne De CARLO - SCARLET ANGEL Ⓤ Tech.
Steve BRODIE, Robert HUTTON - STEEL HELMET Ⓐ
MON., 22 July   In CINEMASCOPE & Technicolor -   For Six Days
● *Prior to London Release* ●
RITA   ROBERT   JACK
HAYWORTH - MITCHUM - LEMMON
FIRE DOWN BELOW
2.45, 5.35, 8.25. Ⓐ
Also —— FULL SUPPORTING PROGRAMME —— L.C.P. 7.35 p.m.

THE GREAT BALLROOM
DANCING NIGHTLY
7.45—11 p.m. - Adm. 3/6 - Late Extensions Thurs. & Sat. - Adm. 4/-
RAY GORDON AND HIS **ORCHESTRA**
Fully Licensed Bars and Lounges
GRAND "GIFT" NIGHTS
Sat., 20 July—Bottles of   THE " SWEET SOMERSET CIDER "
Cider & Babycham at   And " BABYCHAM " DANCE
Mon., 22 July—Channel   ' EAGLE STEAMERS ' NIGHT
Cruise Tickets at
Tues., 23 July   Kleenex   ' KLEENEX TISSUE ' DANCE
Gift Packs at
Wed., 24 July—Boxes of   ' VAN HOUTEN ' Chocolate Gala
Van Houten Chocs. at
Thurs., 25 July—Bottles   ' NICHOLSON'S GIN ' NIGHT
of Nicholson's Gin' at
Fri., 26 July—Amami Bea   'AMAMI' & 'BRYLCREEM' GALA
Packs & Brylcreem at

NIGHTLY at 8 p.m.   Presented by ALAN GALE
Favourite Artistes — Grand New Talent

OLDE TYME MUSIC HALL
● FULLY LICENSED ●
It's " Back to the Good Old Days "
● COMPLETE CHANGE of Programme EVERY TWO DAYS ●
Mr. TED GATTY—Famous Chairman—WELCOMES YOU !
BOOK EARLY for Reserved Tables and Early Door Seats
at the BOX OFFICE, 10.30 a.m.—12.30 p.m. and 3 to 6 p.m.
Ordinary Doors 7.40 p.m. Adm. 1/6. Early Doors 7.15 (Bookable) 6d. extra

Royal Sovereign at Margate. The Thames Estuary was lucky in having some massive resorts that were close to France. From the 1990s onwards, both *Waverley* and *Balmoral* made regular calls at the old pier, recreating steamer services that many thought had disappeared some thirty years earlier.

The *Royal Daffodil* is perhaps the most well-loved of all Thames pleasure steamers. The beauty of her design perfectly suited the modern needs of passengers from her entry into service in 1939 to her sad scrapping in the 1960s. Acker Bilk, Diz Disley, Chris Barber, Monty Sunshine and Kenny Ball frequently performed aboard the *Royal Daffodil* during jazz cruises in the 1960s.

Queen of the Channel arriving at Ramsgate during the 1950s. Ramsgate's fine and impressive harbour was perfect for the vessel, and many passengers would enjoy tea or lunch at the Eagle Café, situated above the landing area. *Queen of the Channel* was over 82 metres in length and could reach a speed of 18 knots. She could carry up to 1,500 passengers.

Royal Daffodil departing from Boulogne. In 1955 *Royal Daffodil* was able to land passengers in France again at Boulogne and Calais. The *Balmoral* made a memorable call at Boulogne from Eastbourne when she operated alongside *Waverley*.

COMBINED RAIL—STEAMER
DAY EXCURSIONS TO
BOULOGNE

WITHOUT PASSPORTS (See page 4)

DAY RETURN FARE 44/-
(including all Pier and Landing dues)

THURSDAYS SATURDAYS and SUNDAYS
28th JUNE TO 16th SEPTEMBER INCLUSIVE

from LONDON (Liverpool Street or Fenchurch Street)
VIA SOUTHEND (Victoria) or SOUTHEND (Central)

OUTWARD JOURNEY (SECOND CLASS RAIL)

		Thursdays	Saturdays	Sundays
TRAIN		a.m	a.m.	a.m.
Liverpool Street	dep.	7A 5	7 15	7A15
Southend (Victoria)	arr.	8 47	8 45	8 58
Fenchurch Street	dep.	7 42	7 42	7 50
Southend (Central)	arr.	8 59	8 59	9 16

STEAMER

Southend Pier	dep.	10 0 a.m.	
Boulogne	arr.	2 0 p.m. (approx.)	

RETURN JOURNEY (SAME DAY ONLY)
STEAMER

Boulogne	dep.	5 0 p.m.	
Southend Pier	arr.	9 0 p.m. (approx.)	

TRAIN
PASSENGERS MAY RETURN FROM SOUTHEND-ON-SEA BY ANY TRAIN FROM EITHER CENTRAL OR VICTORIA STATIONS

Last trains

		Thursdays	Saturdays	Sundays
		p.m.	p.m.	p.m.
Southend (Central)	dep.	10 56	11 0	10 30
		a.m.	a.m.	
Fenchurch Street	arr.	12 11	12 29	11 56
Southend (Victoria)	dep.	10A49	10A49	10A40
		a.m.	a.m.	a.m.
Liverpool Street	arr.	12 24	12 24	12 14

A—Change at Shenfield

CHILDREN UNDER THREE YEARS OF AGE, FREE;

During the 1960s, GSNC could see that day trips and short breaks to the Continent were increasing in popularity. The company reacted to this by introducing a number of coach and rail breaks combined with their sea cruises to France. Dating from April 1956, this handbill outlines combined rail services from Liverpool Street and Fenchurch Street to Southend to catch the GSNC steamer to Boulogne or Calais at the inclusive price of £2 4s. This typically gave three hours ashore in France. No passports were required for the trips.

A fine aerial view of the *Queen of the Channel*. It was common for many of the Eagle Steamer crew members to find lucrative ways of boosting their income. Some were more than happy to arrange an instant table booking and others were known for taking a penny when passengers required the (free) toilet facilities! Up to 1,302 passengers could be carried on her.

G. S. N. Co. Ltd.	General Steam Navigation Co. Ltd.	G. S. N. Co. Ltd.
SUN DECK ENCLOSURE	SUN DECK ENCLOSURE RESERVED FOR HOMEWARD JOURNEY	SUN DECK ENCLOSURE
N⁰ 1116 Homeward Journey to Southend Fee 2/6 DEAL This portion to be retained by the passenger	SOUTHEND DEAL N⁰ 1116 This portion to be inserted in holder on back of Chair	N⁰ 1116 Homeward Journey to Southend DEAL This portion to be given up in exchange for chair

In Festival of Britain year, *Queen of the Channel* was on the London to Southend and Clacton service while the *Royal Daffodil* operated the Gravesend to Southend and Margate service with cruises to the French coast. *Royal Sovereign* ran the London Tower Pier to Southend and Margate run.

Royal Sovereign was launched on 7 May 1948 and undertook her maiden Thames cruise on 24 July 1948 from London Tower Pier to Ramsgate.

Margate Jetty survived until 1979, when it was badly damaged in winter storms. Sadly, the pier was too derelict to be rebuilt and was demolished. The strength of Eugenius Birch's design meant that the demolition process wasn't easy. The entrance was situated close to where the Turner Contemporary Gallery is positioned today.

The film *The Jazz Boat* was extensively filmed aboard the *Royal Sovereign* during 1959. Stars such as Anthony Newley, Bernie Winters, Leo McKern and Joyce Blair were filmed on the ship as Ted Heath and his Orchestra, plus many other musicians of the day, provided music for teenagers. The film showed the stars going on a cruise to Margate with a dramatic climax at Dreamland. The Teddy Boy-inspired movie was directed by Ken Hughes and produced by Albert Broccoli and showed the magnificence of the *Royal Sovereign*.

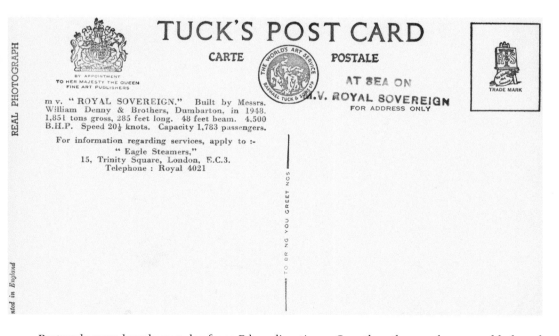

Postcards were hugely popular from Edwardian times. Countless thousands were sold aboard the Eagle Steamer fleet. When posted at sea they were stamped with a special cachet showing the name of the pleasure steamer.

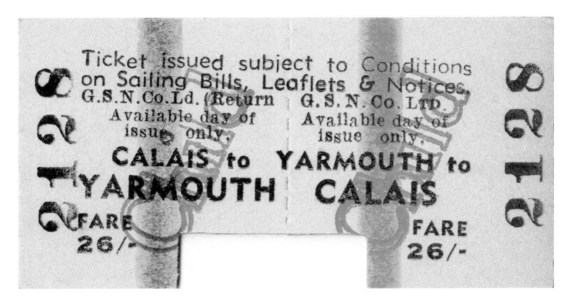

A ticket for the *Royal Sovereign* when based at Great Yarmouth for her final season, when she undertook *26s* day trips to Calais.

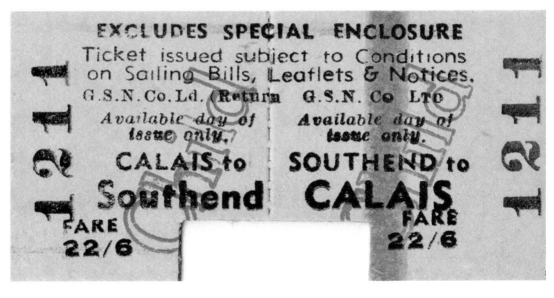

Ticket for a day return from Southend to Calais. GSNC heavily lobbied the government to relax post-war restrictions and to reinstate the cruises to the ports of France with passports. These were a lucrative source of income for the company and it was important that they were reinstated to help halt the decline in revenue.

M.V. QUEEN OF THE CHANNEL

Queen of the Channel photographed on her trials. She was launched at the Denny of Dumbarton yard on 25 February 1949 and was completed for service on 25 May 1949. Her Thames career would last just seventeen years, which was the shortest career of any Thames-specific pleasure steamer.

Royal Sovereign faced an uncertain future when Thames services ceased at the end of 1966. Unlike her sister the *Royal Daffodil*, *Royal Sovereign* was to see further service and in 1967 she was sold to Townsend Brothers, with whom she was converted to carry up to four lorries between Dover and Zeebrugge. She was given the less than majestic name of *Autocarrier* for her new role.

Nº 459

THE GENERAL STEAM NAVIGATION COMPANY, Ltd.

AVAILABLE DAY OF ISSUE ONLY.

TOWER PIER to SOUTHEND (OR VICE-VERSA)

SINGLE.

Does not admit to Sun Deck Enclosure.

THIS TICKET TO BE GIVEN UP ON LANDING.

THIS TICKET IS ISSUED SUBJECT TO THE COMPANY'S CONDITIONS PRINTED ON THEIR SAILING BILLS, LEAFLETS AND NOTICES.

Margate was a perfect destination for the Eagle Steamer fleet and *Royal Sovereign* is depicted in this postcard. The resort provided a great number of large and popular seaside attractions within close proximity the pier. It also allowed passengers to be embarked from the pier for a short cruise along the Kent coastline before the London passengers embarked for the journey home.

Royal Sovereign against Jones & Barry's Tower Bridge, which was built between 1886 and 1894. Each drawbridge weighs 950 tons. Who could ever complain at the start or end of the day when you had a sight like Tower Bridge to greet you?

The lounge deck of the *Royal Sovereign,* showing the great length of the seated accommodation along with the obligatory Lloyd Loom chairs and linoleum floor. No paddle steamer could provide such a long uninterrupted seating space as this.

Royal Sovereign passing Gravesend and Tilbury on 26 June 1965. *Royal Sovereign* was withdrawn at the end of the 1966 season along with the other vessels in the fleet. She was then laid up in Deptford Creek in 1967 before being purchased by Townsend Ferries for £100,000 in that year.

Queen of the Channel at Calais. The jazz boat music cruises seem to have been purely linked to Calais and Boulogne. The GSNC never exploited shorter cruises along the Thames to and from London or the lucrative evening moonlit cruises.

The Winter Gardens Margate   46A

Above: *Royal Daffodil* departing from Margate Jetty. Margate and Cliftonville were lucky as the pleasure steamers could easily be seen quite close to land from the busy palaces of pleasure such as the Winter Gardens and Dreamland. The view of a handsome steamer departing on a cruise to France or along the Kent coast was very enticing and many must have rushed to book a cruise from the nearby booking office.

Right: Towards the end of her career in the early 1960s, the *Medway Queen* required a growing amount of work to ensure that she had an operational future. With dwindling passenger numbers, however, this wasn't possible. Organisers of parties and outings were targeted on this handbill from 1961 to try and increase income. The popular seaside resorts of Southend, Clacton and Herne Bay still provided a good day out from Strood.

10 MAY 1961

To Organisers of Parties and Outings !

BOOK NOW FOR THE 1961 SEASON

(Vessel can be chartered by large parties)

Commencing SUNDAY, 11th JUNE, 1961

Delightful Steamer Trips from STROOD PIER departing 9.15 a.m.

To **SOUTHEND** over 7 hours ashore
DAILY (except Fridays and 17th June)
Depart from Southend 6.40 p.m

To **CLACTON** approximately 3 hours ashore
Every WEDNESDAY and SATURDAY (except 17th June)
Depart from Clacton 4.25 p m

To **HERNE BAY** approximately 4½ hours ashore
Every SUNDAY, MONDAY, TUESDAY and THURSDAY
Depart from Herne Bay 5.00 p.m.

All above Cruises back at Strood approximately 8.30 p.m.

FARES
SOUTHEND 9/-   CLACTON 13/6   HERNE BAY 11/-

Children under 14 half fare.   Under 3 free.   Single and Period tickets also issued

- Fully Licensed Bars
- Attractive Meals and Refreshments served
                                 (Can be booked in advance if preferred)
- Special Arrangements made for Booked Parties
- Car Park adjacent to Pier

For Conditions of Carriage see over

Further particulars and bookings:—   or Agent

THE NEW MEDWAY STEAM PACKET Co., Ltd
ACORN SHIPYARD, ROCHESTER
Telephone Chatham 41355-6-7

R.A.P. LTD   W.72

Royal Sovereign offered impressive facilities for her passengers. In this image you can see the massive sun lounges on two decks with their large windows that enabled day trippers to view the coastline in the dry. There was also more than ample seating on the large open decks for those that required fresh sea breezes. At the bow you can see the deckhands ready to winch the ship in at a pier such as Southend.

Royal Daffodil arriving back at Margate during the 1950s. *Royal Daffodil* was the second Thames and Medway pleasure steamer to bear the name. Her predecessor entered service for the New Medway Steam Packet Company in October 1933, with her being used on the Rochester to Southend route.

The magnificent *Royal Daffodil* in dry dock. She was launched in 1939 and was the ultimate in sophistication and style at the time. *Royal Daffodil's* 1947 refit was completed at the Acorn shipyard at Strood.

"ROYAL SOVEREIGN" LEAVING PIER, MARGATE. K.6254.

When *Royal Sovereign* entered post-war service, she operated the new express London Tower Pier to Margate run. Built by the famous Denny of Dumbarton shipyard, her yard number was 1413. She had a width of 48 feet and had a tonnage of 1,850 tons.

PASSPORT ESSENTIAL

Ticket issued subject to Conditions on Sailing Bills, Leaflets, & Notices

G.S.N.Co.Ltd Return | G.S.N. CO. LTD.

Availabe for Journey | Availabe day of
during the season | issue only

CALAIS to | SOUTHEND to
SOUTHEND | CALAIS

FARE 40/- | FARE 40/-

0419 | 0419

In 1955 restrictions were further reduced and passengers were able to land in France with a passport or an identity card. This made a great difference at the time to the Eagle & Queen Line. One reason why GSNC must have faced a degree of failure in the final years was because they relied almost entirely on the traditional routes and destinations. Places such as Whitstable, Ipswich, Folkestone and Dover were never tested to see whether they would provide new trade and routes.

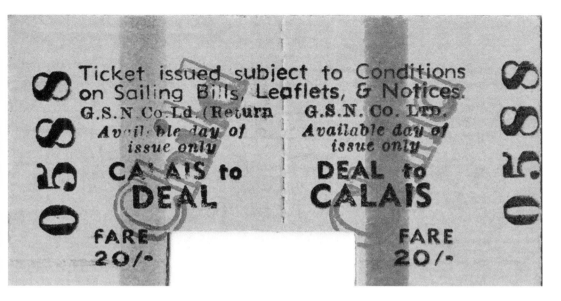

Ticket issued subject to Conditions on Sailing Bills, Leaflets, & Notices.

G.S.N Co. Ld. (Return
Available day of
issue only
CALAIS to
DEAL
FARE
20/-

G.S.N. Co. Ltd.
Available day of
issue only
DEAL to
CALAIS
FARE
20/-

Deal became a regular calling point during the early 1960s for the *Royal Daffodil* and the *Queen of the Channel* on their Calais and Boulogne 'no-passport' trips as well as along the Channel coast to places such as Dover and Folkestone. The 1950s Deal Pier had a very short career as a calling point for pleasure steamers as Thames services ceased nine years after it was opened.

One of the most notable new things to happen to enliven Thames services was the opening of Deal Pier by HRH the Duke of Edinburgh on 19 November 1957. The first pleasure steamer call was by the *Queen of the Channel*. The pier was the last new pier to be constructed in the UK and had a concrete structure. GSNC house flags were placed on the flagpoles at the entrance to the pier.

Deal Pier's extensive landing stage offered GSNC excellent berthing facilities. Queues of eager passengers could regularly be seen along the length of the pier waiting to board a steamer. Nowadays, the mooring bollards are surrounded by men fishing, but the berthing facilities are still more or less as they were in the 1960s. *Waverley* was the last large pleasure steamer to make a call at the start of her Thames career.

Royal Sovereign approaching Southend Pier on 30 July 1950. An arrival at a pier has always meant that almost every passenger crowds the side of the ship facing the pier. There was always a great deal of excitement to see where they would land as well as seeing how many would board the steamer. Such crowding on one side would mean that a steamer would list heavily and that was dangerous as the ship's protective belting could become stuck on the pier timbers.

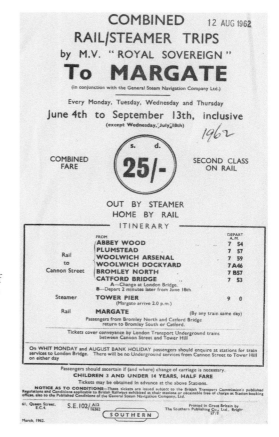

GSNC did all that they could in the early 1960s to attract more passengers at a time of dwindling trade. Combined rail and steamer services were provided aboard steamers such as the *Royal Sovereign*. Passengers travelled to London by train and after a five-hour steamer trip from Tower Pier they could spend as much time as they wanted in the resort before returning by train. This enabled many to have a more flexible day out compared to a couple of hours ashore if they did both legs by steamer.

The lesser-known and second *Crested Eagle* was built in 1938 by Crown & Sons of Sunderland. She was 138 feet long, 25 feet wide and her twin-screw engines could attain a speed of 13 knots.

Crested Eagle at London. She was well known for undertaking the London docks cruises. She could carry up to 670 passengers.

Crested Eagle shown at London having just passed under Tower Bridge. She was on charter to P. & A. Campbell in 1957 for service out of Brighton, Eastbourne and Hastings and never returned to Thames service. Soon after the Campbell charter, she was sold for further service between Malta and Gozo.

DAY TRIPS to FRANCE

With passport, or 3 identical passport-size photographs for special identity card — see page six.

For British subjects and citizens of the Irish Republic, subject to approval of the Home Office and the French Government

Per m.v. "ROYAL DAFFODIL" 2,060 Tons.

EVERY WEDNESDAY 28th JUNE to Mid-September to **BOULOGNE** — on SATURDAYS and SUNDAYS 1st JULY to Mid-September to **CALAIS**

✦ ALLOWING 3 HRS. ASHORE ✦

TIMETABLE

SOUTHEND dep.	9.45 a.m.	SOUTHEND dep.		10 a.m.
BOULOGNE arr. (approx.)	2.0 p.m.	CALAIS arr. (approx.)		2.0 p.m.
" dep.	5.0 p.m.	" dep.		5.0 p.m.
SOUTHEND arr. (approx.)	9.0 p.m.	SOUTHEND arr. (approx.)		9.0 p.m.

N.B.—PASSENGERS ARE REQUIRED TO BE AT SOUTHEND PIERHEAD NOT LATER THAN 30 MINUTES BEFORE SAILING TIME FOR IMMIGRATION AND CUSTOMS FORMALITIES·

DAY **42/-** RET

FARES FOR PARTIES OF 20 OR MORE PERSONS 38/- ADULTS : 19/- CHILD	CHILDREN UNDER 3 YEARS FREE—3 to 14 Yrs.—HALF FARE

WEEK-END RETURN 65/-   SINGLE 37/6d.   PERIOD RETURN 75/-
(PASSPORT NOT ESSENTIAL)   (PASSPORT ESSENTIAL)
(OUT SAT.—HOME SUN.) Bicycles or Tandems SINGLE 10/- ; RETURN 20/-

FULLY-LICENSED CATERING

ATTENTION IS SPECIALLY DIRECTED TO REGULATIONS ON PAGE 6.
ADVANCE BOOKING RECOMMENDED

2

On **MONDAYS, TUESDAYS & THURSDAYS**
26th JUNE until Mid-SEPTEMBER

m.v. "ROYAL DAFFODIL"

will sail

at **10** a.m.

to allow 5 hours ashore at

MARGATE

Day 15/6 return

Single 10/-   Period Ret. 17/6
CHILDREN—Under 3 Yrs.—FREE   3 to 14 Yrs.—HALF FARE

3 hours ashore at

DEAL

Day 17/- return

Single 11/-   Period Ret. 18/6
CHILDREN—Under 3 Yrs.—FREE   3 to 14 Yrs.—HALF FARE

or the grand 9 hours

FRENCH COAST CRUISE

Fare 21/-

CHILDREN—Under 3 Yrs.—FREE   3 to 14 Yrs.—HALF FARE

TIMES

SOUTHEND dep. 10.0 a.m.		DEAL dep. 4.15 p.m.	
MARGATE arr. 12.15 p.m. (approx.)		MARGATE dep. 5.30 p.m.	
DEAL arr. 1.15 p.m. "		SOUTHEND arr. 7.30 p.m. (approx.)	
7.30 p.m. SOUTHEND to GRAVESEND—Single Fare—5/-.			

FULLY-LICENSED : RESTAURANT SERVICE and LIGHT REFRESHMENTS

3

DAILY Fridays excepted 27th MAY to Mid-SEPTEMBER
(NO SAILING ON SUNDAY, 25th JUNE)

m.v. "ROYAL SOVEREIGN"

Sails at 12.0 noon—to allow 2 hrs. at

MARGATE

Day Ret. 13/-   :   Period Ret. 17/6   :   Single 10/-
CHILDREN—Under 3 Yrs.—FREE.   3 to 14 Yrs.—HALF FARE.

TIMES

SOUTHEND dep. 12.0 Noon	MARGATE dep. 4.0 p.m.	
MARGATE arr. 2.0 p.m. (approx.)	SOUTHEND arr. 6.0 p.m. (approx.)	

6.0 p.m. to LONDON (Tower)   arrive 9.0 p.m. (approx.)

SINGLE FARE 9/-

FULLY-LICENSED   :   RESTAURANT SERVICE & LIGHT REFRESHMENTS

On **SUNDAYS**   9th & 23rd July   6th & 20th August

The 1,500 tons Cross-Channel Ship

"QUEEN of the CHANNEL"

will leave the Pierhead

at **2.45** p.m.

FOR A FINE TWO HOURS TRIP

UP THE RIVER MEDWAY

Adult 6/- fare

CHILDREN—Under 3 Yrs. Free   3 to 14 Yrs. HALF FARE

Arriving back 4.45 p.m. and sailing at 5.15 p.m. for

MARGATE	DEAL	RAMSGATE
arr. 7.15 p.m. (approx.)	arr. 8.30 p.m. (approx.)	arr. 9.00 p.m. (approx.)

FARES

SINGLE 10/-	SINGLE 11/-	SINGLE 11/-
PER RET. 17/6	PER RET. 18/6	PER RET. 18/6

FULLY-LICENSED : CAFETERIA CATERING—TEAS, etc.

4

A special feature in 1961 was four Sunday afternoon trips up the River Medway by the *Queen of the Channel*. Passengers from Deal, Ramsgate and Margate could do this cruise. The *Royal Sovereign* offered cruises from London to Southend then onwards to Margate.

— 4 MAR 1961

EAGLE STEAMERS

(The General Steam Navigation Co. Ltd.)

Programme *of* Sailings
from Southend *pier*
to

BOULOGNE	**CALAIS**
MARGATE	**DEAL**
HERNE BAY	**CLACTON**
FRENCH COAST CRUISE	

and

4 SPECIAL SUNDAY AFTERNOON TRIPS

UP THE RIVER MEDWAY

All sailings, times, etc., are subject to weather and other circumstances permitting.

BOOKING OFFICE
PIER HILL, SOUTHEND-ON-SEA

Telephone 66597 (May/Sept.)

Local Manager   A. A. Mundy

See Page 6 for Conditions of Carriage and important notes.

1

A programme of cruises from Southend Pier in 1961. This was a replacement paper programme for the normal pocket-sized booklet. The cruises finished on Sunday 10 September in that year.

The small motor vessel *Crested Eagle* moored up for the winter on 19 September 1952 with the GSNC vessel *Woodcock* astern of her. This view shows the modest size of the *Crested Eagle*, which was well suited to the popular local London docks cruises.

Clacton Pier with the *Queen of the Channel* alongside towards the end of her Thames Estuary career during the 1960s. Clacton's wide pier has always included a plethora of rides, swimming pool, penny arcades and cafés due to its considerable width. However, it was affected by navigational issues such as numerous and extensive sandbanks further out to sea, making it less accessible than Southend and Margate. Nevertheless the resort offered a lot for passengers, although never on a par with Southend or Margate.

Medway Queen departing from Southend Pier for Herne Bay in July 1959. Her withdrawal in 1963 helped to focus on the demise of pleasure steamers. Many people joined together to try and preserve the heritage of pleasure steamers for future generations to enjoy. This ultimately led to the operation of *Waverley, Balmoral* and *Kingswear Castle.*

Queen of the Channel at Calais. On the way to France the three motor ships passed the wartime forts that were used as pirate radio stations. Sometimes the ship's crew would retune the ship radio, where DJs such as Screaming Lord Sutch would welcome the vessel from his radio station on Shivering Sands Fort. His pirate radio career was short-lived and during his time at sea he would advertise local shops in Whitstable.

Above: An aerial view of the *Queen of the Channel* at Boulogne. The final years of GSNC saw the company equipped by pleasure steamers that, although fine and luxurious, were clearly too large to be economic. It was sad that smaller vessels weren't purchased for new or traditional routes. Even the catering had hardly changed in more than half a century, and passengers were now becoming used to foreign and convenience food. The cruises to France were made in an attempt to boost flagging trade, but maybe the answer lay elsewhere, or maybe it was just too late.

Left: A brochure for new services to Boulogne from Gravesend and Southend. The trip from Gravesend, which took five hours and twenty-five minutes, offered passengers three hours ashore to soak up the Continental atmosphere of France.

Royal Daffodil departing from Boulogne. During the outward trip, passengers were able to book additional coach tours to Wimereux and Wissant at an additional cost. Visits to the First World War cemeteries were popular for many decades for folk wishing to see where their relatives were buried.

Queen of the Channel at the Paradise Bassin at Calais. She was unique in that she operated on a Friday, which was the traditional Thames off-service day. Instead, her off-service day was Saturday.

Queen of the Channel at Boulogne. The year 1959 was one of wonderful sunny summer weather and GSNC naturally had one of their most lucrative seasons ever. The only drawback for GSNC was that the no-passport trips to France didn't show an increase. This was inevitable though, as competition from the ferries was beginning to bite.

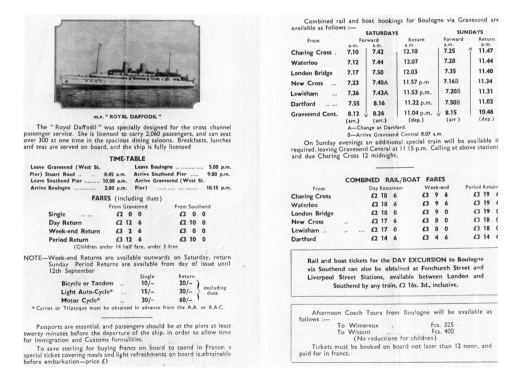

m.v. " ROYAL DAFFODIL "

The " Royal Daffodil " was specially designed for the cross channel passenger service. She is licensed to carry 2,060 passengers, and can seat over 300 at one time in the spacious dining saloons. Breakfasts, lunches and teas are served on board, and the ship is fully licensed

TIME-TABLE

Leave Gravesend (West St.)   Leave Boulogne .... 5.00 p.m.
Pier) Stuart Road ..   .. 8.45 a.m.   Arrive Southend Pier ..... 9.00 p.m.
Leave Southend Pier .... 10.00 a.m.   Arrive Gravesend (West St.
Arrive Boulogne .... 2.00 p.m.   Pier) .... 10.15 p.m.

FARES (including dues)

	From Gravesend	From Southend
Single	£2 0 0	£2 0 0
Day Return	£2 12 6	£2 10 0
Week-end Return	£3 2 6	£3 0 0
Period Return	£3 12 6	£3 10 0

(Children under 14 half fare, under 3 free)

NOTE—Week-end Returns are available outwards on Saturday, return Sunday Period Returns are available from day of issue until 12th September

		Single	Return	
Bicycle or Tandem	..	10/–	20/–	} excluding dues
Light Auto-Cycle*	..	15/–	30/–	
Motor Cycle*	..	30/–	60/–	

* Carnet or Triptyque must be obtained in advance from the A.A. or R.A.C.

Passports are essential, and passengers should be at the piers at least twenty minutes before the departure of the ship, in order to allow time for Immigration and Customs formalities.

To save sterling for buying francs on board to spend in France, a special ticket covering meals and light refreshments on board is obtainable before embarkation—price £1

Combined rail and boat bookings for Boulogne via Gravesend are available as follows :—

	SATURDAYS		SUNDAYS	
From	Forward a.m.	a.m.	Return a.m.	Forward a.m.	Return p.m.
Charing Cross .	7.10	7.42	12.10	7.25	11.47
Waterloo	7.12	7.44	12.07	7.28	11.44
London Bridge	7.17	7.50	12.03	7.35	11.40
New Cross ...	7.23	7.40A	11.57 p.m	7.16B	11.34
Lewisham ...	7.26	7.43A	11.53 p.m.	7.20B	11.31
Dartford	7.55	8.16	11.22 p.m.	7.50B	11.02
Gravesend Cent.	8.12 (arr.)	8.26 (arr.)	11.04 p.m. (dep.)	8.15 (arr)	10.46 (dep.)

A—Change at Dartford.
B—Arrive Gravesend Central 8.07 a.m.

On Sunday evenings an additional special train will be available if required, leaving Gravesend Central at 11 15 p.m. Calling at above stations and due Charing Cross 12 midnight.

COMBINED RAIL/BOAT FARES

From	Day Excursion	Week-end	Period Return
Charing Cross	£2 18 6	£3 9 6	£3 19 6
Waterloo	£2 18 6	£3 9 6	£3 19 6
London Bridge	£2 18 6	£3 9 0	£3 19 0
New Cross ..	£2 17 6	£3 8 0	£3 18 0
Lewisham	£2 17 0	£3 8 0	£3 18 0
Dartford	£2 14 6	£3 4 6	£3 14 6

Rail and boat tickets for the DAY EXCURSION to Boulogne via Southend can also be obtained at Fenchurch Street and Liverpool Street Stations, available between London and Southend by any train, £2 16s. 3d., inclusive.

Afternoon Coach Tours from Boulogne will be available as follows :—

To Wimereux . . Fcs. 325
To Wissant .. . Fcs. 400
(No reductions for children)

Tickets must be booked on board not later than 12 noon, and paid for in francs.

Royal Daffodil was built for cross-Channel service. Over 300 people at a time could be seated in her luxurious dining saloon. For £1 you could take your bicycle with you and for £3 you could take a motorcycle. In those days before mobile phones you could make a three-minute UK telephone call from the ship for 10s 6d.

For many passengers, a trip on one of the GSNC pleasure steamers was a highlight of each summer. Many chose to buy a small souvenir of their trip aboard the steamer to use at home during the year. The company produced a wide range of bottle openers, caddy spoons and tea strainers showing small enamel images of the three vessels.

Royal Daffodil at Boulogne. The no-passport trips to France were doing great business throughout the post-war years. There were 61,300 passengers in 1957, 78,500 in 1958, 77,164 in 1959, and 78,031 in 1960.

Queen of the Channel at Calais. *Queen of the Channel* and the *Royal Daffodil* had quite similar patterns of operation in the initial post-war years. In 1956 the need for having the three large motor ships was obvious when the number of trips with passports doubled to ten a week from five in the previous year.

Queen of the Channel was laid up at the end of the 1966 season. Initially it was thought that she had a future as a pleasure steamer as she was a fair bit smaller than the *Royal Daffodil*, but this never materialised. Her sister the *Royal Sovereign* was not at all suited as a year-round cross-Channel ferry when she operated as *Autocarrier* in her second career. Passengers were often made aware of this. She earned the nickname of the 'Townsend Submarine' as a result!

Between 1963 and 1965 the three splendid pleasure steamers *Royal Daffodil, Royal Sovereign* and *Queen of the Channel* continued their familiar pattern of operations but with a few minor tweaks. By this time it was clear that the pattern of change was irreversible and that whatever the mighty GSNC tried to do to halt the decline it would only have modest success. In 1965, GSNC introduced a service to Barcelona whereby the *Royal Daffodil* carried passengers from Gravesend, Tilbury and Southend to Calais. From there they travelled by coach to Paris and then by coach again to Barcelona. The trip was obviously very long and tiring. The trip took thirty-six hours in each direction and cost £20 15s per adult. Although a novel idea, it would never be a huge success. It was rumoured at the time that GSNC wanted to develop this service further in competition to the cross-Channel ferries and the growing appetite for holidays in Spain. The experiment was doomed to failure, however, as it was undertaken too late.

Queen of the Channel looking majestic at Boulogne. At the end of the Second World War the Eagle & Queen Line steamers had house emblems placed on their funnels. *Royal Daffodil, Royal Sovereign, Royal Eagle* and *Golden Eagle* had the GSNC red and white house flag, while the *Queen of the Channel* and *Medway Queen* had the New Medway Steam Packet house flag, featuring the rearing horse of Kent. When the *Medway Queen* was withdrawn in 1963, the *Queen of the Channel* received the GSNC house flag on her funnel.

Rochester Queen alongside the inner berth of Clacton Pier in the 1960s. This aerial view shows that Clacton Pier must be the widest pier in UK. Passengers disembarking from the *Rochester Queen* must have been bombarded by countless sideshow owners and penny slot machines as they walked along the pier. The swimming pool was a very popular attraction, as well as the ballroom at the end of the pier.

At Southend, vessels such as the *Queen of the Channel* aroused a great amount of anticipation in their passengers as the steamer gave panoramic views of the coastline and attractions such as the Kursaal and Peter Pan's Playground as they arrived at the pier. No car could give such an exciting view.

Queen of the Channel was initially laid up at Rochester on the River Medway from 1966 until being sold in 1968, when she was sold for further service at Piraeus in Greece. She was renamed *Oia* for this role, and in 1976 was then renamed *Leto*. *Queen of the Channel* met her end in August 1983 when she arrived at Eleusis in Greece for scrapping, which started on 29 March 1984.

Southend regularly offered trips to Margate, whereby passengers could make their outward journey on one ship and return on another. The pier train at Southend could at times outshine London commuter trains. On Whit Monday 1948, 45,000 passengers were carried on it to and from the pier head. A major factor of the 1966 cessation of Thames services was the Seamen's Strike of 1966. A result of this was the loss of the first six weeks of the summer season. In 1966, the *Royal Daffodil* was strike-bound in Calais, and as a result she was unable to carry out her early season service of taking French schoolchildren from Calais to London, returning them a week or so later after their holiday in London was completed.

The Londoner at Calais. The demise of Thames services by GSNC was dealt a huge blow by the arrival on the Thames of the ferry *The Londoner* in 1965. This was a combined car and passenger ferry and was swiftly placed on the Tilbury to Calais route. Passengers were able to enjoy a fine Scandinavian smorgasbord along with bingo and undercover facilities that were largely denied them on the GSNC vessels. They could also take their car with them.

Royal Daffodil at Boulogne. In 1966 the regular London Tower Pier to Southend and Margate service was confined to the most lucrative days of Saturdays and Sundays. *Royal Sovereign* was also placed at Great Yarmouth for her first cross-Channel services to Calais as well as operating the Thursday Clacton to Calais run. *Royal Daffodil* and *Queen of the Channel* shared the Gravesend, Southend, Margate and Deal trips to France. *Queen of the Channel* also operated the weekend trips from London Tower Pier to Southend and Margate.

Queen of the Channel alongside the wharf at the Courgain at Calais. GSNC never exploited upriver cruises to London from the resorts of the Kent and Essex coasts in the post-war years. The company purely saw their services as serving the Kent and Essex seaside resorts, as well as Calais and Boulogne. It was an aspect of potential business that may have opened up new markets in the 1960s.

Deal's pier had been closed to pleasure steamer traffic since 1914, so the availability of the new 1957 pier at this famous and attractive resort was a real boost to GSNC. *Queen of the Channel* is making a call in this view.

Queen of the Channel alongside at Calais towards the end of her Thames career. She was often under the command of Captain Stoddard, who was known for his high standards as well as his calm personality.

Queen of the Channel at Calais. The arrival of *The Londoner* on the Thames in the mid-1960s was the final death blow for the GSNC fleet. Although the new ferry service was short lived and only survived for around a year after GSNC left the Thames, it had shown the once invincible GSNC that Thames passenger services had changed forever and that the decline was inevitable and couldn't be reversed.

By the mid-1960s, GSNC realised that the heyday of Thames pleasure steamer services was at an end. They could see that the future lay in ferry services and that the familiar, well-loved resorts of Margate, Southend and Ramsgate were no longer economic calling points. The end for GSNC on the Thames came on 20 December 1966 when they announced the cessation of Thames services and the three famous and well-loved vessels *Royal Daffodil*, *Royal Sovereign* and *Queen of the Channel* were immediately put up for sale. It was quite simply the end of an era. The *Royal Daffodil* was the first casualty of GSNC's demise. Her departure was filmed by the BBC, who showed her journeying to her execution under the breaker's torch up the Terneuzen Canal in Belgium. *The Daily Telegraph* produced a similar sad final departure story. Unlike the *Medway Queen's* withdrawal, the demise of the Thames motor ships wasn't met with the same deluge of protest as most folk thought that they would find a new role as ferries, seeing as they were more or less new vessels and had been in service for less than twenty years. Sadly, the lack of protest meant that all three Thames pleasure steamers departed for sad futures, with them becoming barely recognisable from their heyday on the Thames in those glorious post-war years. Christmas 1966 marked the end of a remarkable period. The memories created during those carefree post-war years could never be repeated. There have been many attempts to recreate the services and atmosphere of those decades but nothing has ever come close to the distinct and special atmosphere of the *Royal Daffodil*, *Queen of the Channel* and *Royal Sovereign*. Memories created by them will always remind former passengers as well as future generations of times before the internet and motor car, when the simple pleasure of a cruise to the seaside aboard a comfortable and luxurious ship was part of everybody's life each summer. Those decades of pleasure may never be repeated.